CAPTURED!

INSIDE THE WORLD OF CELEBRITY TRIALS

MONA SHAFER EDWARDS
COURTROOM ARTIST

TEXT BY JODY HANDLEY

SANTA
MONICA
PRESS

Published by:
Santa Monica Press LLC
P.O. Box 1076
Santa Monica, CA 90406-1076
1-800-784-9553
www.santamonicapress.com
books@santamonicapress.com

Printed in China

Santa Monica Press books are available at special quantity discounts when purchased in bulk by corporations, organizations, or groups. Please call our Special Sales department at 1-800-784-9553.

ISBN-13: 978-1-59580-011-4
ISBN-10: 1-59580-011-5

Library of Congress Cataloging-in-Publication Data

Edwards, Mona Shafer, 1951-
  Captured! : inside the world of celebrity trials / by Mona Shafer Edwards ; text by Jody Handley.
    p. cm.
  ISBN 1-59580-011-5
1. Edwards, Mona Shafer, 1951---Themes, motives. 2. Courtroom art--United States. 3. Celebrities--United States.
4. Trials--United States. I. Handley, Jody. II. Title.

NC953.8.E39 A4 2006
741.973--dc22

2005033238

Cover and interior design by Future Studio

Front cover illustrations: Top (left to right): O.J. Simpson, Robert Blake, Winona Ryder, Michael Jackson
Middle: Sergeant Charles Duke demonstrating a chokehold on attorney Ira Salzman during the Stacey Koon/Rodney King trial
Bottom (left to right): Courtney Love, Alec Baldwin, Richard Ramirez, Michael Eisner
Title page illustration: Courtney Love raises her hand to ask a question of the judge, while her attorney, Michael Rosenstein, stands at her side
This page: Attorneys Nancy Lucas, Peter Ezzell and Eric Dubin watch Robert Blake describe how he kept his gun in his boot
Back cover illustrations: Top (left to right): Catherine Zeta-Jones, Snoop Dogg
Middle (left to right): Rodney King, Farrah Fawcett
Bottom (left to right): Mel Gibson, Clint Eastwood

CONTENTS

ACKNOWLEDGMENTS

This book is dedicated to my adored, chic, and brilliant father, Dr. Joseph Shafer. He instilled in me the love of news, the excitement of the Story, and the curiosity to find out as much as possible about people. He would have adored these tales.

My thanks to my dearest mother, Marie Dawidowicz Shafer, whose prescription for living, "Head up and forward," has been a constant guide. I am forever grateful for her artistic talent and style.

My children, Marc and Marisa, have had their childhoods marked by sometimes gruesome and scary stories of my days in court shared at the dinner table. I thank them for putting up with me, and forgiving me my passions!

My lovely and accomplished literary agent, Joy Tutela, from the David Black Agency in New York, worked tirelessly to find the perfect fit in a publisher and writer for me. A quintessential West Coast book put together by a proper Bostonian!

Jody Handley "got it" in one meeting in San Francisco, and I thank her for her dry wit and putting together beautifully written portraits to fit my pictures.

Jeffrey Goldman and Amy Inouye, with flair and amazing vision, have been wonderful to work with, and have created exactly the book I had always envisioned.

Much appreciation to my friends at KABC News and the people on the assignment desk who have kept me busy since 1985. Those last-minute phone calls make my days exciting!

Thanks also to Howard Levine of CDS Photo and Graphics. Lee Lindenlaub has been my best friend, dog-walking partner, biscotti and cappuccino pal, and gossip-sharer for the last six years. She has encouraged me to do this book since we met. Thank you!

Finally, I want to mention my husband, Barry, dearest friend, harshest critic and sharpest business lawyer. . . . With a good eye, and infinite patience, he can give the best critique of any art professor I ever had, and he can't even draw. Thank you for enduring so many years of insecurities and animal obsessions.

One of the attorneys representing Allergan, Howard Weitzman, questions Irena Medavoy on the stand

The scene in the federal
courtroom at the trial of former
Mouseketeer Darlene Gillespie

INTRODUCTION
THE ART OF
THE COURTROOM SKETCH

Of the thousands of trials going on every day throughout the country, only a select few grab and hold the attention of the nation for days or weeks on end, and those are, by and large, trials that feature a celebrity. Even stories of the rich and powerful in New York can't compare with those of a sitcom star in Los Angeles. If celebrities are America's royal family, then L.A. is London, and Hollywood is Buckingham Palace. Which would make *me* a royal court artist, I suppose. As a courtroom sketch artist in L.A., I've drawn some of the most famous faces of the past few decades, capturing many of them at their most vulnerable moments.

About 25 years ago, while working mainly as a fashion illustrator, sketching for department store catalogues and newspaper advertisements, I began studying courtroom illustrations on television. They struck me as stiff, amateurish—no flair, no pizzazz, nothing that would make me believe the people involved in the case were *real*. Fashion emphasizes speed, knowledge of anatomy and movement, and most importantly, *style*—that special quality that makes a viewer look twice. I convinced the art director at an L.A. news station to let me prove my worth, and in no time I turned my markers away from the fashion police and towards the L.A.P.D.

My first case was *Triola v. Marvin* in 1979. In a nutshell, Michelle Triola sued her former live-in lover because he had said he would care for her for the rest of her life. The case became a landmark one—it established that cohabitating lovers can sue on pillow-talk promises if all aspects of an oral contract are established and fulfilled (i.e., palimony law).

Not necessarily exciting stuff in and of itself. But add in that the "Marvin" in question was *Lee* Marvin, star of *The Dirty Dozen, The Big Heat,* and dozens of other films, and you have a media frenzy.

My life changed as a result of that case, and it hasn't been the same since. For nearly 25 years, my daily life has had no predictability. I keep a suitcase full of clothes and art supplies in the trunk of my car so that I can be at an arraignment at a moment's notice. Usually, my calls arrive early in the morning, when news stations schedule time slots for the evening newscasts. I might drive two hours to witness a five-minute hearing, or drive ten minutes to cover a trial that lasts

months. Most often, I illustrate the defendant's first arraignment or appearance, opening statements, closing arguments, and the verdict. Only trials with a "marketable angle" warrant full-time coverage, and usually the media decides what's marketable. (Sometimes a case catches my eye and I convince my assignment editor that it'll hit big. When a man threw his young, rich wife overboard from his powerboat, the case drew little media attention, but I begged to cover it. In the end, the public embraced it for all its sex, power, infidelity, and money. You'll find the details in *People v. Eric Bechler*.)

Depending on the trial, I draw anywhere from two to seven or eight sketches in a day. During the Michael Jackson's molestation trial, for instance, every network in the country had constant feeds

Jack Klugman listens to testimony of his former flame, Ms. Neuglass

going, so during each break the stations wanted something new. I did my best to keep up with them, sometimes churning out six or seven sketches in a day. My hand cramps occasionally, but usually it's more from tension than overwork. If I know I'm losing my model in just a moment and my sketch isn't finished, I white-knuckle the pen until my fingers cramp.

At the moment, only one other courtroom illustrator is my friendly competitor in L.A., and we often work as complements to each other. We compare sketches, cover for each other when one can't be in court, and take turns when only one artist is allowed in the room. We both love our work, and we both pray for the "no cameras permitted" rule from the judge.

I sit in the front if I can; occasionally I move around to get the best angle, or if there's no jury and the judge allows it, I may sit in the jury box. Sometimes the judge assigns us seats; for Michael Jackson, O.J., and the Menendez brothers—all media circuses, for instance—we

had assigned seats (usually with a bad view). I carry about 50 markers and pens—and generally use about 5—and a pad of 9″ × 12″ vellum paper. I often manipulate the ink from the oil-based markers with my finger to add dimension, and try to draw both from photographic memory and with speed. I never erase; I

use a blade to scrape off marker (that is, when the bailiff allows me to bring a blade into the courtroom) and I've gotten more than a few quizzical looks from people who wonder what the scratching noise is. I only use a certain kind of pen, and I buy them by the dozens at a time. When I find a brand name I like, I depend upon it, and

if someone goes out of business, I panic, so I tend to buy my supplies in bulk.

My best sketches are my fastest, the ones in which I capture a brief, emotionally intense moment and lay it down in minutes. I never know how much time I'll have, so I have to get the image on paper as quickly as possible; three min-

utes is usually my goal. I tend to over-work the sketch if I have too much time, and I prefer the lighter, fresher look of spontaneous sketches—it's kind of the California style. New York artists have a heavier look—they're the oil paintings to our watercolors. Maybe it's the weather. Neither is the "correct" way, of course. For me, the longer I spend on filling in a sketch, the more I dislike it—my first impression, both to my eyes and to the page, is usually the best.

I never use a pencil, and I never make a loose sketch. I usually have the sketch finished in my mind's eye before I even put the pen to paper. I start with an eyebrow, or where the eye meets the bridge of the nose, and build out from there. I try to capture body language, the hairline, a particular expression; hands are one of my greatest inspirations, because they're so indicative of mood. Hands around the face, clasped beneath the chin, praying—they all contribute to the character of the piece.

Avoiding "caricature" is one of the hardest parts of my job, especially when

I'm drawing famous faces. It's not always easy to keep from exaggerating the likes of Michael Jackson. And I always have to remind myself to draw the person in the room, not the one on the screen. I know what Farrah Fawcett looks like before I even see her, but I have to be sure to do an interpretation of her in the moment. Years

of experience have taught me to sense those impending moments—when Robert Blake falls over, ill; when O.J. Simpson demonstrates "wrassling" with Nicole with clenched fists . . . these are the times when my pen's practically quivering in my hand.

Once I finish my sketch, the media "buys" the right to photograph it—

that's how I earn my living. During the short breaks in the cases, I tape my translucent vellum sketch to a white bristol board, run downstairs to a camera truck, and fasten the sketch to the nearest vertical item, whether it's a car or a tree. The camera people shoot the picture, usually panning from side-to-side to give

Catherine Zeta-Jones on the witness stand

Heather Locklear on the witness stand during Hunter Tylo's trial with photos from her appearances on *Melrose Place*

the illusion of movement (I make a point of placing my sketches off-center to help them out), and then I zip back upstairs to catch the next chapter. Not surprisingly, we also sell our work to attorneys, who spend willingly, as courtroom sketches are a common gift for some lawyers. L.A. attorney Mark Geragos—defender of Winona Ryder and Michael Jackson (until Jackson replaced him one week before his arraignment)—told me he calls his collection of sketches his "ego wall." Once, a drug lord asked me to sell him a sketch. I declined.

Objectivity is always a goal of any documentarian, but I can tell you this now: no documentarian can be 100% objective. After all, we're not automatons. I try to avoid interpreting the trial, but I often play up a specific moment that seems relevant—for instance, during the Rodney King case, I drew one of the defendants praying with his wife before

the trial, an extremely emotional moment. My own emotions also occasionally come through on the paper, in the background colors I use, in the boldness of the strokes. Sometimes people realize they're being drawn and they duck their heads, hold up papers, do anything to avoid my line of sight. No one wants to be drawn in their moments of greatest vulnerability, and some moments—for instance, verdicts, when I am focused on the reaction of the family and the defendant—are especially difficult.

Of course, sometimes the attention of a courtroom artist is *exactly* what someone wants. Some people become more theatrical when they're being watched. Attorneys often ask me to make them look a bit thinner, or give them more hair; after all, image is everything, especially in this town. By the time the jury exits the room for the last time, I can arrange my drawings in order and follow the tale of the

trial, from arraignment to verdict.

Seeing these cases week after week has jaded me somewhat, no doubt. My mother swears I've become more hardened, but the bottom line is, I just see things most people don't ever witness. I'll be driving down the freeway and an image—from that week, or years earlier—will jump into my head and then sit in my soul for weeks before I can let go of it. Seeing the cases has also softened me a bit, too. We're all flawed humans who have unsavory impulses from time to time. In the end, though, all my sympathy for a defendant won't change the fact that he or she is guilty. And in my opinion, some people can be just plain evil.

My job does bleed over into my personal life. I have never been on jury duty, and I doubt I'd be selected. I know nearly every judge, D.A. and bailiff in the county, after all. Last year, my husband and I saw burglars leaving our neighbor's house and wrote down their license plate; we may be asked to testify in court, and I wonder if I'll be expected to draw myself. Naturally, I'm always hoping I'll never draw anyone I know. (It's a common joke between me and my friends: Don't let me

sketch you, please!)

At the end of the day, I love my job; I believe my colleagues and I are the keepers of an important, though dying, art. While I can remain unobtrusive and disappear, every person in a courtroom is aware of a news camera. I've seen attorneys exaggerate their "performances" for the camera, and judges and witnesses inevitably look self-conscious when faced with the glass eye. What I find to be most valuable about drawings, though, is the humanity they convey. Drawn by a human hand, perceived through a human eye, they bring an emotional reality to a captured moment—a reality that can be lost in the starkness of a video camera.

Courtroom illustration is a unique, irreplaceable art form, used to seize a moment in criminal history. Any courtroom can be a fascinating place, but my courtroom is located in the heart of the glamorous, scandalous City of Angels, which, for me anyway, makes my work that much more compelling. Join me now on a journey through the surreal world of the famous, the infamous, the notorious—the celebrity crime.

JEANNIE ADAIR
I WISH THEY ALL COULD BE CALIFORNIA BLACK WIDOWS

People v. Jeannie Adair (1999)

Attorney Richard Plotin demonstrates baseball bat grips while his client, Jeannie Adair, watches. The police sketch of the "gas company worker" in the background.

Sometimes, the most interesting cases don't involve celebrities—until the defendants become celebrities themselves, at least for a short while. Such is the case of Jeannie Adair, who was accused of beating her husband to death with a baseball bat in 1996.

Saucer-sized blue eyes, blond wavy hair, rosy lips—Jeannie Adair was the quintessential California girl. The day her husband, Robert, was murdered, she said a man in a gas company uniform came to her door, forced his way inside, and beat, bound, and gagged her in her bedroom. As the man ransacked her apartment, stealing her jewelry, her husband returned home from lunch; she heard thuds, the closing of the screen door, and then nothing. When she freed herself from her bonds, she found her husband in a pool of blood and raced outside for help.

The police suspected the story as soon as they arrived on the scene. Adair described several hours of "ransacking" in her condo, but the apartment was too neat for the typical burglary. Plenty of valuables were left over; the bed where she was hog-tied was barely touched; her wounds could have been self-inflicted. Perhaps most telling, Robert Adair had two $200,000 life insurance policies—and Jeannie had cheated on him the previous year.

Adair pointed the finger at Mindy Shapiro, the wife of Adair's orthopedic surgeon and former lover, Michael Shapiro. Mindy said Adair did it. Michael said Mindy did it. And no one ever tracked down the mysterious gas compa-

affairs (that testimony was barred). While the prosecuting attorney said the direction of the blood spray, away from the killer, meant Jeannie's clothes could be clean, the prosecution's own expert witness said blood *would* be found on the killer.

When the prosecutor offered opening statements, Jeannie sat there, stoic and serious, big blue eyes wide with gravity; when her attorney presented the case, she cried her eyes out. Personally, I think the judge had a bit of a crush on her. Meanwhile, Robert Adair's mother aged 20 years.

THE VERDICT

Not guilty. After three days of deliberations, the jury found Jeannie Adair not guilty because of reasonable doubt. She expressed her regrets that the murderer was still at large by saying, "I don't feel I can really celebrate. The people that did this to my husband are still out there, and not until they are behind bars and charged with this murder will I be happy." (The prosecutor accused her of "taking a line from O.J. Simpson.") Shortly thereafter, Jeannie dumped the highway patrolman she had been dating throughout the case.

ny man. Two years after the murder, Jeannie Adair was arrested.

Throughout the trial, defense attorney Richard Plotin built a case of reasonable doubt: Mindy had connections to the Mafia and a brother in prison, she had written threatening notes to Jeannie in the past, and Robert Adair

was a victim of being in the wrong place at the wrong time. Mindy, on the other hand, said Jeannie and Michael had conspired to commit insurance fraud, claiming Michael operated several times on Jeannie's same injury.

The prosecution's case fell apart with each witness placed on the stand.

Michael Shapiro's assistant said Jeannie called during the time she was supposedly hog-tied, yet when Shapiro testified, he said it could have been his wife who called. Jeannie's coworker said the defendant had injured herself on the job in order to receive worker's compensation and insurance, and had several other

CAPTURED!

Jeannie Adair watching testimony of former flame Dr. Michael Shapiro

Simone Adair (sister of Robert) testifies

Judge Wiatt looking at Jeannie Adair, wearing black and sobbing

Jennifer Aniston and husband Brad Pitt
(bearded for a film) in court

JENNIFER ANISTON PRETTY NAKED GIRL!

Jennifer Aniston v. Francois Navarre (2002)

Boundaries can be a bit fuzzy at times, and I don't just mean the boundaries of good taste. Sometimes, real property boundaries can be fuzzy—is it okay to climb a tree and snap topless photos of your neighbor? If you sell those photos to international skin magazines—and that neighbor is Jennifer Aniston—the answer is, most emphatically, no.

I assume Francois Navarre, stalkerazzi extraordinaire, thought he was well within his legal rights to scale an eight-foot wall overlooking the *Friends* star's backyard and zoom in with his telephoto lens. Just as he figured there was no problem with selling the photos to Man's World Publications (publishers of *Celebrity Skin*) and the Crescent Publishing Group (*High Society*), who, in turn, published the photos. *High Society*'s headline read, "Rachel Gets Raunchy: Her Shocking, XXX-Rated Vacation."

Actually, she wasn't on vacation, she was in her own backyard; and the raunchiness consisted of the star chilling in her backyard wearing only her panties. After settling for an undisclosed amount with several international publishers, Aniston went after Navarre himself, suing him for invasion of privacy.

She looked just lovely in court, even fully clad (no visible tan lines, either). New husband Brad Pitt accompanied her to court, with a full beard and long, unkempt hair—presumably for a movie role. She wore a simple white blouse and slacks, her hair in a ponytail, and the pair painted the picture of marital bliss and solidarity. The courtroom was, of course, packed, and after Jennifer and Brad left the court, the judge announced that his feelings were hurt—no one had come just to see him.

Jennifer Aniston in Judge
Ronald Lew's federal courtroom

THE VERDICT

Guilty. The court awarded Aniston $550,000 in damages. Navarre issued an apology and paid $100,000; his insurance carrier covered the remaining $450,000. The newlyweds split up in 2005, and as of this printing, Brad Pitt is hitting the tabloids with new flame Angelina Jolie, while Jennifer has been seen in the arms of actor Vince Vaughn.

Charts of the Secret Garden restaurant interior are displayed for the jury

Randy Valli watches as friend Frankie Avalon demonstrates to the court how his chair was yanked at the Secret Garden restaurant

FRANKIE AVALON
BIG GIRLS DO CRY

People v. Randy Valli (1999)

As if former child stars don't have it bad enough, former teen idols seem to have a knack for getting into scrapes, too. Or in this case, their wives do. When crooning duo Frankie Avalon and Frankie Valli took their wives out to dinner at the Secret Garden restaurant in 1999, they walked away with a lot more than the flavors of Provence. The pair saw the outrageous prices—$30 an entrée—and complained to the owner, Sandra "Alex" Sofsky, who was not keen on being told her food wasn't worth the price.

A squabble followed, which soon escalated into a skirmish, ending with Frankie Valli's wife, Randy, slapping Sofsky—and Sofsky suing for misdemeanor battery. I sat in court the day Frankie Avalon testified, and his testimony was, in the words of he and Annette, a

gas. He said they fled the restaurant in terror, that Sofsky screamed obscenities at them, shaking Randy's chair until Randy waved her arms around. She didn't slap her, he said; she "accidentally pushed" the owner. Randy later said Sofsky shook the earring out of her ear, and snapped her bra strap, to boot.

THE VERDICT

Guilty. Randy was convicted of misdemeanor battery, and, proving that sometimes big girls *do* cry, she burst into tears at the declaration. As for Frankie Avalon, he's aged quite gracefully, his pompadour still standing proud, and has that charming affability that won him the hearts of so many bobbysoxers. Before the trial started, he even sent a check to the restaurant to cover the cost of the bill.

Avalon does "show and tell" for the attorneys and judge

Alejandro Avila at his murder trial

Sarah Ahn shows prosecutor where her playmate, Samantha Runnion, was kidnapped

ALEJANDRO AVILA INNOCENCE LOST

People v. Alejandro Avila (2005)

This case was, in a word, heartbreaking. Every shred of evidence, every witness, everything about this case just crushed me and everyone else in the room; few things are as tragic as a child's death, but the violation of a child is one of them.

On the evening of July 15, 2002, a man approached five-year-old Samantha Runnion and her friend Sarah Ahn as they played in her front yard. "Have you seen my Chihuahua?" he asked, and as Samantha answered, he snatched her and dragged her, kicking and screaming, to his car. Sarah was left with a remarkably vivid impression of the man, providing police with a near-perfect description of him for the sketch.

Just a day later, a child's body was found and identified as Samantha's. Not only had she been sexually assaulted, asphyxiated, and beaten, but she was found in an oddly posed position. The manhunt for her killer began, and with the help of Sarah's description and callers' tips, police located Alejandro Avila, a production line supervisor who had lived in Samantha's complex in the late 1990s. He had been previously arrested for molesting two young girls, but was acquitted on all charges.

The case was like a real-time episode of *CSI*; everywhere police turned, they found new evidence supporting their case against Avila. Samantha led the police directly to her captor: his skin was under her fingernails. This little girl lived up to her motto of "Be brave"—she went down fighting. In the most heartbreaking evidence, the police found her tears all over the inside door of Avila's car.

In his defense, Avila tried to say the scratches on his legs were from a baby gate at his family's apartment; the

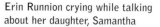
he wanted her to dress like a little girl. He told her he loved little blonde blue-eyed girls, which, coincidentally, happened to be exactly what her daughter looked like. He also refused to have his feet uncovered; he even wore socks in the shower.

The ex-girlfriend's daughter, one of the girls Avila had been arrested for molesting, took the stand along with several other teenagers. Avila worked in a medical supplies factory, and he would bring home test tubes and insert them in the girls' vaginas, telling them it would prepare them for "bigger things"; the testimony was, quite simply, nauseating.

And throughout the entire trial, young Erin Runnion, mother of a remarkably beautiful child, sat behind Avila, and said nothing. She never screamed or lashed out, although she did cry from time to time. For having been through hell and back, to hear what had happened to her daughter and not break down, was a brave thing, indeed. She was a perfect lady.

The only time Alejandro Avila showed *any* emotion was when his mother had a seizure on the stand and had to be removed by ambulance

prosecution brought experts to say baby gates couldn't create those kinds of scratches. As if the physical evidence wasn't enough to nail him, the prosecution brought in a parade of witnesses to testify against him, ranging from his sisters to ex-girlfriends to the little girls he had been previously accused of molesting. The defense, perhaps hoping he

would at least be spared the death penalty, tried to paint him as a victim, a poor child whose dad abandoned him; when they showed a picture of his father holding him as a baby, he wept. His aunts and uncles had sex around him, the defense said, and the family engaged in all manner of perverse acts—this made him into a victim, not a predator.

Several witnesses struck me in particular. Sarah, Samantha's friend, used a teddy bear to show where they were standing and what happened during the abduction. Avila's ex-girlfriend also testified, saying he had wanted her to dress younger, and she thought that meant she needed to look hip. It turns out he meant pinafores and jumpers—

THE VERDICT

Guilty. I sat next to one of the sheriffs during the verdict, and I was stunned by the outpouring of relief and grief that coursed through the room. These officers had seen the case through from start to finish, and they cried when Avila was found guilty; days later, we all wept when Erin Runnion read the most thoughtful, dignified, touching witness impact statement I'd ever heard:

"Since Samantha's death I have felt more hate and rage than I ever thought possible, but I love that little girl so much that it would be a horrible insult to her to let my hate for you take more space in my heart and head than my love for her."

We all cried again when he was sentenced to the death penalty. I don't remember the last time I sat through such a brutally raw, emotional case, and I hope I don't ever have to go through it again.

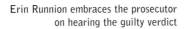

Erin Runnion embraces the prosecutor
on hearing the guilty verdict

25

Court reporter feigns pulling her hair out
because of Baldwin's rapid-fire speech

ALEC BALDWIN
CELEBRITY GRUDGE MATCH

Alec Baldwin v. Alan Zanger (1998)

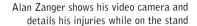

Alan Zanger shows his video camera and
details his injuries while on the stand

When Alec Baldwin and wife Kim Basinger brought home their new baby daughter in 1995, they were greeted by a van across the street. Suspecting that the van's owner also owned a video camera, Baldwin sprayed the windows with shaving cream. "Celebrity stakeout specialist" Alan Zanger leapt from the truck, video camera in hand, and in the ensuing confrontation, Zanger's nose was broken. After both parties dialed 911, and the L.A.P.D. arrived, Zanger made a citizen's arrest.

Those are the facts. The truth is a bit fuzzier. Baldwin says Zanger lifted his camera in a menacing manner, and when he slapped away the camera in self-

Alec Baldwin shows how he struggled
with videographer Zanger

defense, it accidentally hit Zanger's nose and knocked off his glasses. Then, he said, Zanger attacked him. Zanger, on the other hand, insisted that an enraged Baldwin punched him without provocation.

In true Hollywood style, the trial seemed to be decided from the moment Baldwin took the stand. I've never seen such a perfect witness, someone who so typified his matinee idol status. He smiled at the jury, and his testimony was firm, intelligent, eloquent, charming, and funny. Like the native New Yorker he is, he spoke so quickly at times that the court reporter couldn't keep up. Eventually, her frustration drove her to feign pulling her hair out. Baldwin apologized to the reporter profusely, simultaneously diffusing the courtroom's natural tension and winning us over.

Zanger, on the other hand, embodied Baldwin's direct opposite: he

Alec Baldwin charms the court reporter

Attorney presenting Baldwin's video of paparazzi Zanger approaching car

was not handsome, sympathetic, or smooth, and his job was so distasteful—especially considering the fact that he sought out the couple on their homecoming from a childbirth—that he came off as pesky paparazzi. Though his stress seemed genuine, it wasn't enough to convince the jury.

THE VERDICT

Not guilty. Baldwin was acquitted of misdemeanor battery, a verdict that rang out like a church bell to other celebrities plagued by paparazzi. Also in true Los Angeles style, the story doesn't end there:

Zanger followed up by filing a civil suit against Baldwin, charging him with assault, battery, emotional distress, and the loss of an estimated $200,000 in income.

"I'm a wreck, I'm apprehensive every time I do something," Zanger said. "I can't do my work like I used to."

Baldwin countersued Zanger for invasion of privacy, negligence and distress. In 1998, the jury awarded damages on both sides for negligence claims, and in the end, Baldwin had to pay Zanger $4,500 in damages—a small price to pay for a movie star who just wants to be left alone.

Alec Baldwin showing photos
of his car and Zanger's truck

A few years later, I sketched Baldwin and Basinger in court again, but under sadder circumstances. They battled over the custody of their eight-year-old daughter in 2004, and I found myself sketching these two remarkably beautiful people, sitting at the same table, three lawyers between them, and refusing to look or speak to each other. Basinger's father cited Baldwin's fiery temper as the primary reason for the divorce. The paparazzi apparently aren't the only objects of his anger.

Baldwin's lawyer accuses Basinger of preventing phone conversations and visits with the couple's daughter, November 2005

ERIC BECHLER
A WATERY GRAVE

People v. Eric Bechler (2001)

Eric Bechler watches his
attorney, John Barnett

Sometimes, a case pisses me off. Sometimes it's the verdict, sometimes it's the witnesses, but once in a while, the accused is such an appalling person that just breathing the same air as him infuriates me. Such was the case with Charles Rathbun, who murdered model Linda Sobek in 1995; such was also the case with Eric Bechler.

During the summer of 1997, Pegye Bechler headed off the coast of Newport Beach with her husband, Eric. She was probably thrilled—her handsome young husband had planned a romantic anniversary celebration on a chartered boat. A few hours later, Eric sobbed in front of television cameras, telling the tragic tale of a party gone awry.

Tina New testifies against
former boyfriend Eric Bechler

Pegye had disappeared into the ocean. They had been waterskiing (kind of a boogie board version of it); Eric fell off his board and went underwater. When he surfaced, Pegye was gone and the boat was circling.

Pegye's friends and family suspected Eric immediately. They knew the marriage was going sour, and probably never trusted the former beach bum who had enchanted their friend. Pegye had had a successful physical therapy clinic, but after her wedding to Eric, the Bechlers soon found themselves on the verge of bankruptcy. But that didn't stop them from living the ideal life of beach dwellers in Orange County—volleyball games on the sand, attending parties at every house in the neighborhood, and enjoying a view of the Pacific from their back porch.

Once the police began investigating the disappearance, however, evidence

Eric Bechler watches his
attorney, John Barnett

Eric Bechler on the stand,
with photo of the boat where
he and Pegye went for a picnic

piled up like empty beer cans at a barbe-
cue: Blood was found in the boat. Eric
began collecting on several insurance poli-
cies. Two weights were missing from his
weight collection, something that's always
amused me. Picture it: one of those big tri-
angular weight racks, all of the weights
clearly visible and displayed, with two
obvious blank spaces. You would think
someone with the forethought to charter a
boat and concoct a story would've
thought to cover up the "MISSING
WEIGHTS HERE" sign in his own house.

    After Pegye's disappearance and
Eric's tearful performance before the cameras, he seemed to recover quickly. He
began carrying on with Dennis Rodman's
ex-girlfriend, Tina New. After one night's
drunken confession to her, she contacted
the police and agreed to wear a wire for
her next date with Eric.

    The plan worked. Over dinner,
Eric proclaimed how he loved Tina, how
he wanted to create a beautiful life with
her, and how he had killed his former
wife. What woman wouldn't be charmed
by such a swell guy? The police nabbed

The weight rack, as evidence,
with one missing

FRANK F. FASEL
JUDGE

CAPTURED!

A friend and neighbor of Pegye Bechler
testifying about volleyball parties on the beach

him immediately, and Eric wasted no time in hiring John Barnett, a top trial attorney.

Eric's arrogance came off of him in waves, especially at first (I suppose a crate of evidence humbles even the most experienced sociopaths; he was anything but arrogant toward the end). He never cried, or expressed sadness or loss, even when the defense played him as the poor, beleaguered widower. When the prosecution described how they suspected he slit her open, stuffed her with weights, wrapped her in plastic, and dumped her overboard, he appeared to be watching a vaguely interesting episode of *Law & Order.*

Pegye's mother, on the other hand, came to court every day, wearing pins and ribbons in her daughter's memory. Tina was very pregnant and married, and while she reminded me of Anna Nicole Smith, I think we all sympathized with her. Eric had charmed an intelligent, successful businesswoman like Pegye; he clearly knew his way around a woman's mind.

(An interesting sidebar: there was some question about whether the case was state or federal, since the police couldn't decide if the crime had been committed in Californian or Mexican waters. They eventually determined that she had been killed in California, and drifted into Mexico.)

As you've probably noticed, the parallels between this case and the Laci Peterson case are striking; I often wonder if Scott didn't take a few cues from Eric. Which probably wasn't so wise, considering how things ended for Eric.

THE VERDICT

Guilty. Eric was sentenced to life without parole. I spoke with Pegye's mother after the verdict, and she was thrilled with the outcome, of course. It was a sad case, indeed, but in the end, justice was served.

Becker's attorney shows leash that was used to tie up his client

Marcelle Becker demonstrates how she was restrained by her dog's leash while on an American Airlines flight

MARCELLE BECKER
THE MALTESE PUPPY DOG

Marcelle Becker v. American Airlines (1999)

Cases like this always have me imagining a screenplay pitch to a producer. I pitch the movie, and the producer says, "What, are you kidding me? No one would believe that." *Marcelle Becker v. American Airlines* might possibly be one of the most ridiculous cases I've ever witnessed—which is what makes it so darn fun to share with you. While the name Marcelle Becker may not be immediately recognizable, believe me when I say this case is as L.A. as it gets, bringing together the wounded pride of a wealthy widow, a major American airline, a hissy fit, and a dead Maltese dog named Dom Perignon.

On July 6, 1995, something happened on a flight from New York to Los Angeles. Both sides agree on these facts: Becker, who sat in first class with Dom Perignon, her Maltese, let the dog out of its Louis Vuitton carrying case. A flight attendant told her dogs roaming free on the flight were not permitted, and asked her to put the dog back in the case. Then some kind of altercation erupted; the old dog died sometime after the flight, and Becker sued the airline for assault, battery, violation of civil rights, and cruelty to animals.

The "altercation" is where the details get fuzzy. Flight attendants and even the pilot say Becker was unreasonable, thus interfering with the flight. The defense said Becker had had two alcoholic drinks and half of a Xanax. Evidently, the depressants didn't work because witnesses said she also threatened to kick out the windows and kill everyone on board. The pilot eventually restrained her with the only tool he had handy: Dom Perignon's leash.

Becker, on the other hand, testified that the pilot punched her in the stomach and kicked her while the attendants restrained her with a chokehold. Then they assaulted her dog as well, before tying her up. The assaults on Dom Perignon resulted in $7,000 in medical costs for the animal, she said, but he still died within months of the flight.

The airline employees seemed more frustrated than anything else, being dragged from their jobs to participate in a ludicrous lawsuit for a plaintiff who needed money like she needed a submarine. Becker, on the other hand, was always perfectly coiffed, arriving each day with bodyguards and her public relations man in tow; arrogance came off her in waves. I don't doubt that she grieved for her lost pet, but would more money bring him back?

THE VERDICT

Not guilty. In March of 1999, a jury rejected her claims of mental and physical abuse, and no damages were paid. In 2000, Becker filed suit against her attorney, Jerry Kaplan, for legal malpractice; the suit was dismissed two months later.

Robert Blake at his first appearance in court

Judge Darlene Schempp watches Prosecutor Shellie Samuels question stuntman Ronald "Duffy" Hambleton

ROBERT BLAKE WISEGUYS

People v. Robert Blake (2005)

Sometimes, even a dramatic murder trial can have its light moments. The case seems absurd, the reporters are relaxed, the defendant's an updated version of Jimmy Cagney, and even the sheriff's deputies are begging for an invitation to the wrap party. Between the colorful witnesses, the trips to the murder scene, and a general camaraderie among the media and police alike, the nine weeks of the trial just seemed to fly by.

In late May of 2001, every news station scrolled a bizarre headline: "Wife of *Baretta*'s Robert Blake Shot to Death." The reporters threw around words like "execution-style" and "criminal history"; in a scene yanked from a 1970s Mafia film, Blake's wife was shot inside her car, outside of an Italian restaurant. Her grieving husband told the cops of the Lurking Stranger, a man who had been seen around their home in Studio City.

Here's where the entertainment begins.

The presence of the Lurking Stranger had set the couple on edge, Blake said, so he began carrying a handgun all the time. His worry was so intense, in fact, that he had forgotten the handgun in the restaurant and had to return for it. Just as he stepped into the restaurant to retrieve the very thing that would protect his wife, the Lurking Stranger emerged from the darkness to execute Bonny Lee Bakley, 45. Oh, irony, thy name is forgetfulness!

Perhaps suspecting his story wasn't April-fresh, the police did a little questioning and turned up a few more gems. Bakley's half brother, for instance, said Blake had said she "already had a bullet with her name on it" long before her murder. The police turned up letters from her lonely-hearts scam; one involved swindling an 82-year-old widower out of $250.

(Apparently she wasn't upholding her end of the prenuptial agreement, in which she swore not to break any laws.) And then there's Bakley's one daughter—Blake's, as proven by DNA—and three other children with her ex-husband (though she claims one is Jerry Lee Lewis's daughter).

It took almost a year, but in April of 2002, the L.A.P.D. arrested Robert Blake for the murder of his wife, and his chauffeur/bodyguard for conspiracy to kill Bonny Lee Bakley. The defense was simple enough: Hey, everyone hated her. Anyone could've done it.

ODE TO GRECIAN FORMULA

Jail is like a time machine for some people. Without a daily dose of cosmetics, defendants are suddenly thrust forward into time, sometimes twenty years or more, so we can see what they *really* look like. Blake's age and apparent vanity only enhanced the process. The first thing to go: his hair.

His arraignment presented a handsome man with black hair styled into a pompadour. Stuntmen came forward to say Blake had tried to hire them as hitmen; the pompadour fell into a flop.

Blake watches his daughter, Delinah, talk about money in her father's home

L.A. wrapped its smoggy arms around the case and embraced it. Vitello's, the Italian restaurant at the scene of the crime, carried his favorite dish, the "Robert Blake Special"—fusilli with spinach (execution-style killing not included)—for years, so every tourist enamored with *The Sopranos* or *Baretta* could order it. One detective asked me if I'd be so kind as to not draw him bald; I compromised by making him a gift of a bald paper doll with an attachable Elvis pompadour.

METH MONSTERS AND DUST FAIRIES

The prosecution presented a parade of witnesses describing Blake's phony cries for help at the crime scene. (You would think an actor would've realized crying for help was the role of a lifetime. Or the role to prevent a lifetime sentence, in any case.) One prosecution witness, a former *Baretta* stuntman, said Blake had asked him to "pop" his wife; on cross-examination, he admitted he had been using cocaine and marijuana heavily, had spent time in a psychiatric ward, and had lied under oath the previous year. Blake allegedly asked another stuntman to "take care of" his wife; under cross-examina-

The bodyguard's grocery list, including such tasty items as pool acid, lye, and shovels, was entered as evidence; an ever-widening skunk's stripe appeared at the part in his hair. By October of 2002—Blake's second denied request for bail—he had cut off the last vestiges of his youth and revealed a white-haired man that looked like he had lived all 67 years with a cigar in his mouth and a tumbler in his hand. (See my series of sketches, which I call "Ode to Grecian Formula.")

One day, in a vaguely surreal move I'll never understand, he showed up with no eyebrows. He had shaved them. The more I draw someone, the more I get to know them, and the better their sketches turn out; but how am I supposed to draw a guy with no eyebrows?

Let's grab a ride on that time machine and skip through two years of preliminary hearings, pretrial proceedings, and jury selection. It's now December, 2004. Blake's on his third lawyer. The case has, at long last, come to trial. I've been drawing Blake for two years off and on, and finally the payoff: a roomful of reporters, photographers, and courtroom attendees who found the case as bizarre and obvious as I did. And who, naturally, equally enjoyed the antics of the witnesses.

Bonny Lee Bakley's daughter, Holly Gawron, testifies at the Blake trial

tion, it was revealed that this second stuntman lied to the police after the murder and had been using methamphetamines for quite some time.

Just to cement the incredibility of the prosecution's primary witnesses, the defense then led in the most motley crew of witnesses I've ever seen. Meth addict after meth addict took the stand—each "tweeker" with fewer teeth than the one before, each one looking like he or she had just crawled out of someone's basement. They had all spent time at the stuntman's ranch in Lancaster, a desolate place in the high desert, and they all described the ample amounts of crystal meth they had crushed and snorted with the prosecution's key witness. One

described a wild night of romping in the desert and hiding from the "four-foot-tall horned creatures."

To top it all off, the defense brought up a psychiatrist from U.C.L.A. to say that many meth users mistake bushes for animals—sometimes horned creatures, in fact—and they believe that tiny fairies live under the couch (I believe they're called "grinlings," or something similar). And this shrink would know; he had devoted his career to studying the effects of drug abuse, and he even possessed a cadre of crack-addicted monkeys in his lab. Between the dust fairies, the Seuss-like desert creatures, and the cracked-out monkeys, I've never seen so many journalists trying not to laugh out loud.

Blake sat behind his table, patting his hair.

Bring on Frank Minucci, an old friend of Blake's from the neighborhood back East. A former numbers-running, loan-sharking mobster, he had since given his life to the Lord and cut out the "bad guy stuff." His testimony was a joy to behold: Blake was led around by his "hooza-whatzi," Minucci said, and refused to use profanity. As Minucci left the courtroom, he told reporters, "This guy's a dirtbag. You don't kill the mother of your children."

Blake patted his hair.

He wasn't always so cool, though. One day, as I drew him, I noticed a thin veil of sweat on his brow; his complexion

turned cheesy and his eyes, glassy. I leaned over to writer Dominick Dunne and said, "He's going to collapse." I thought he had had a heart attack, but he may have just been nauseated; vomit played a key role in the trial. Apparently, Blake vomited before and after the murder, and the prosecution tried to say that proved his guilt. Nope, said the defense team—Blake vomited all the time.

No high-profile murder trial is complete without a visit to the crime scene, and, standing before Vitello's, I noticed an unusual number of bystanders in crisp white shirts—every actor-waiter in the restaurant had come for a chance to be on television. And no wonder—the street was like a movie set, with a full reenactment of the evening's events. The lawyers rented the same make of car and dumpster and waited for the time at which the light would be similar to the evening of the shooting; police lined up along barricades, holding back bystanders walking their dogs in the dark, cold evening. And me? I was hired to draw the faceless jury and scene. I stood beneath a streetlight to get every shred of light I could for the drawing.

Blake? He kicked back, a cigarette perched behind one ear.

couldn't erase that shred of reasonable doubt. Without thanking the jury, a traditional move for a recently acquitted defendant, Blake turned and walked out of the courtroom, and then told a reporter to shut up at the news conference. What a swell guy.

A few months after we finished the first draft of this book, Blake's civil trial began. I'd call it O.J. redux, except that I don't think O.J. seized control of the courtroom before losing $33.5 million. At one point during Blake's appearance on the stand, the judge started to remove his robe, handed it to the wise guy, and offered to let him officially run the trial. I've never before seen a defendant object to a lawyer's comments *from the stand*—or, for that matter, sustain the objections from his own lawyer. Not since Maria Shriver had anyone shown that kind of control in a courtroom, and she was a wilting violet compared to Blake.

My favorite moment, though, and the reason I've decided to add a few paragraphs, is the Skittle story. I'd been watching Blake for nearly a year in his trials, and one thing I'd realized was that he was charming, entertaining, and oddly sympathetic. He has the vocabulary of a Depression-era street kid—which, of course, he was—and he's very

The trial just spiraled at that point. A costar of Blake's from *In Cold Blood* testified. Blake showed up wearing a pinstriped suit that may have been expensive when he starred in *Baretta*. Actors, stuntmen, waitresses—the trial was more Hollywood than any I've ever drawn. Even the judge got in on the action: An attractive and low-key woman, her hair went from frizzy to wavy to a soft pageboy during the course of the trial.

BACK TO THE SCENE OF THE CRIME

On the last night of the trial, the courtroom crew—an assortment of media folk—all gathered at Vitello's to celebrate the strange bond we had all forged over the past few years. Surrounded by red tablecloths and fake plants, eating the mediocre Italian food that was more abundant than appetizing, we planned the wrap party I'd be hosting and traded imitations of meth-snorting mobsters. Late in the evening, a waitress approached me

and said, "You look really familiar."

"I've been drawing you for the last month," I said.

The next day, a deputy asked if he would be getting an invite to my wrap party. The prosecutor, on the other hand, sent her regrets: she would be attending a Bob Dylan concert that evening.

THE VERDICT

Not guilty. Despite all the evidence, despite three months in the courtroom, despite everything, the prosecution

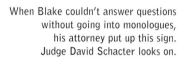
Watercolor of nighttime scene during jury visit

When Blake couldn't answer questions
without going into monologues,
his attorney put up this sign.
Judge David Schacter looks on.

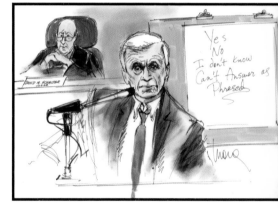

intelligent. We also had something in common: we both draw. I noticed his legal pad was covered in a sketch of a ranch, complete with horses and pine trees; on one tree, he etched "Bobby Blake." He never had much of a childhood, and he still sketches wilderness fantasies like a Boy Scout who never went camping. (He also collects toy soldiers and sleeps with a cap gun under his pillow, but I digress.)

Blake started calling me the "artist lady" at one point, and approached me during his civil trial to pay me a compliment.

"Hey, artist lady," he said, "I been watching you. Your work's good. The other artists make me look like Gabby Hayes on a bad day."

"I noticed you draw," I said. "Were you able to draw while you were in jail?"

He did, he said—he got a little 3-inch pencil, and used a shaver on the edges to sharpen the pencil.

"Did you do any watercolors?"

"My lawyer did nothin' for me," he snorted. "But I learned a few tricks."

Turns out the other inmates taught him how to make his own watercolors. Get a pack of Skittles—not M&Ms, because they melt into chocolate—moisten a cotton ball or tissue, and then dab the Skittles with your finger or, if you're lucky enough to have one, a paintbrush. Other inmates used them for makeup and decorating shirts; Blake used his water-color paintings as barter.

I was oddly touched by his story, that he tried to create something of beauty in such a place. The next day, of course, he showed the courtroom how he kept a gun in his boot. You can take a man off the streets, but . . . well, you know the rest.

Eight months after the first verdict, the jury in the civil trial, after prolonged deliberations, found Blake liable for intentional murder and awarded Bakley's four children damages of $30 million.

JIM BROWN
HOW TO BEAT YOUR WIFE'S CAR WITH A SHOVEL

People v. Jim Brown (2000)

Sometimes a case is so teeth-grindingly frustrating that I want to shake someone. In this case, I wanted to shake Monique Brown. And then I wanted to hug her.

On the night of June 15, 1999, she called 911 to report that her husband, ex-football-star Jim Brown, had taken to smashing her car with a shovel. He had threatened her life, she said, although he hadn't hit her. "Not today," were her exact words, which confirmed the dispatcher's suspicion of a history of domestic violence. No less than seven police cars reported to Brown's residence and the star was arrested for domestic abuse.

This was not Brown's first violent outburst off the football field. As an 18-year-old, he was accused of rape, but was later found innocent. He was accused of throwing his girlfriend from a balcony in 1968, but she refused to testify, and the charge was dropped. He was acquitted of assaulting a man after a traffic accident in 1969, and he spent a day in jail after beating up a golfing partner in 1979. In 1985, he was charged with rape, sexual battery, and assault, but those charges were also dropped due to the accuser's inconsistent testimony. Only a year later, he was arrested for beating his fiancée for flirting with other men; when she didn't want to prosecute, he was released.

History repeated itself in 1999. After her shaken 911 call, Monique refused to testify against him. She appeared at Jim's side on *Larry King* two months after the call, saying she never felt as though she was in danger. Monique said she wanted to withdraw the charge, but given Jim's history, the prosecution followed through with their must-arrest policy. After O.J. Simpson, the L.A.P.D. wanted to take no chances with reported abuse cases—hence the seven cars reporting to Brown's house.

Monique Brown on the stand
while her husband looks on

Prosecutor showing how Jim Brown
may have wielded shovel

Once the trial started, Monique was like a little lamb. We waited on tenterhooks for her to say something, anything, indicating that Brown was not the perfect husband, but no—she sat there, arms folded, staring at him with big eyes, waxing poetic on his loyalty and love as a husband as the prosecution played the 911 tape and described how he pounded her car with a shovel. It was all her fault, she said. She had incited it. Meanwhile, he sat at the defense table, forearms like hams, listening as his quiet wife excused his every transgression. He also blamed the incident on PMS; apparently, they never fought when she wasn't on her period.

The real excitement, though, came outside the courtroom. Mobs of women's defense groups crowded the parking lot, deriding him and screaming at her. She didn't stand up and represent abused women, they said; she turned her back on domestic violence when she was in a perfect situation to speak out on it. At the end of each day, Brown, kufi cap perched on his brow, would speak in front of the courthouse, surrounded by brothers of

Jim Brown with his wife

the Nation of Islam, calling himself a victim of racial persecution. "I'm a catalyst to represent all these people that have been unjustly prosecuted by the system," he once proclaimed.

Brown insisted that the police forced his wife to say she had been abused. He also claimed that the female judge, Dale Fischer, hated men and belonged to an extremist group opposed to minority men. (In actuality, the American Inns of Court, the "extremist group," has many black members, and three blacks on the board.) Meanwhile, the women's groups screamed and shouted at him, waving their placards.

THE VERDICT

Guilty of vandalism. Judge Fischer sentenced Brown to a year of domestic violence counseling, three years of probation, and 40 days of community service. Since Brown's conviction was vandalism, he objected to the counseling; he also said the community service was nothing more than an attempt to make him into a slave for the court. He refused to meet the terms of his sentence and was thus sentenced to six months in prison—a move he said made him a "political prisoner." Monique remains his staunch defender, comparing him to Nelson Mandela and Martin Luther King, Jr., in a 2002 interview; she even suggested that taking out his aggression on the car, not her, was a positive step for Brown.

As for those of us who attended her trial, well, I'm just hoping, for her sake, that I'll never have to draw Jim Brown in court again.

Playing the 911 tapes

Football great Jim Brown sobs while watching his wife testify on his behalf

FIRST DEGREE
FELONY
MURDER

• THE unlawful k...
  human being
• Whether inten...
  unintentional.
• ...

Ennis Cosby Murder Trial 1998

ENNIS COSBY AMERICA'S FAMILY

People v. Mikhail Markhasev (1998)

Rare is the case when a celebrity is the victim, not the accused; in this case, Ennis Cosby wasn't really a celebrity in his own right. His dad was, though—and after watching *The Cosby Show* for years on television, we all felt like we knew Ennis. He may not have been Theo Huxtable, but we felt a kinship with him. And we all loved his dad.

On the night of January 16, 1998, Cosby was on his way to visit a friend, Stephanie Crane, when his tire went flat. He called Crane, and she arrived on the scene, switching on her headlights so he could change his tire in full light. She waited in the car for her friend.

Moments later, a man arrived, banged on her window, and demanded she open the door or be shot. Crane locked the door and drove away; the would-be robber moved on to Cosby and demanded money; when the young man didn't move fast enough, the robber shot him in the head and fled the scene. When Crane returned to the scene, she found her friend dead, lying in a pool of blood.

The outpouring of grief was immediate and intense. We all felt like we had lost a childhood friend, or the friend of one of our children; we saw Theo Huxtable grow up, and by proxy, Ennis. (Theo's storyline often followed Ennis's life—they were both dyslexic, for instance.) Crane's description resulted in a police sketch plastered all over Southern California, but it still took two months to find their man: Mikhail Markhasev, a Ukrainian immigrant and former gang member with a record. Police believe he was looking for drug money when he killed Cosby.

Crane couldn't identify him in a lineup, but the prosecution still had a case: DNA evidence, Markhasev's own letters

Mikhail Markhasev at his arraignment

The Markhasev family, with Victoria,
mother of defendant, on the right

Markhasev being addressed
by Judge David Perez

saying it was a robbery gone wrong. The primary defense? They had the wrong guy—Markhasev was framed by fellow gang member Eli Zakaria. The sketch could be Zakaria, after all, and two prosecution witnesses—gang members who negotiated their story with the *National Enquirer*—weren't exactly credible.

Throughout the trial, my heart went out to the families. Bill Cosby showed up for the closing statements and verdict alone, and he and his wife Camille created a stark contrast to Markhasev's mother and grandmother, who came every day. The Cosbys wore a united front, a strong face; they said nothing, showed little emotion—driven, I imagine, by extraordinary grief and a refusal to provide fodder for the tabloids. "Forget me and my feelings," Cosby did say at one point. "I'm talking about the victim."

The Markhasevs, on the other hand, let their emotions out; they were defensive, visibly upset, and were the antithesis of the Cosby's quiet stoicism. The two mothers, though, had one tragedy in common: they fiercely loved their sons, and while one had already suffered a great loss, a similar loss seemed to be in store for the other.

THE VERDICT

Guilty. The sentence: the 19-year-old immigrant would spend the rest of his life behind bars without chance for parole. In February of 1999, a judge refused Markhasev's request to grant a new trial. And the Cosbys' lives go on.

Snoop Doggy Dogg. Murder Trial

SNOOP DOGGY DOGG
GANGSTA COOL

People v. Calvin Broadus and McKinley Lee (1996)

Snoop Doggy Dogg, a.k.a. the king of West Coast gangsta rap, a.k.a. Calvin Broadus, is possibly one of the most impeccably groomed defendants I've ever seen. He's certainly one of the coolest—meaning he exuded utterly relaxed confidence, conscious of the courtroom full of fans, and fairly unaffected by the charge he faced: first-degree murder.

In a West Los Angeles park in 1993, Phillip Woldermariam was shot and killed by Snoop and his bodyguard, McKinley Lee. That they fired the shots that killed him was not at issue—self-defense was the question in this trial. Defense attorneys argued that Snoop fired shots from his Jeep after the rival gang member attempted to pull a weapon from his waistband.

Sitting directly behind the rapper, I couldn't help admiring the perfectly plaited, smooth braid hanging from his head. He and his entourage—and I do mean entourage—all wore elegantly tailored designer suits, and they all appeared as though they were making an appearance at an awards show, rather than a murder trial. He signed autographs, nodded to his fans, and showed little concern about the pending verdict.

THE VERDICT

Not guilty. A mistrial was declared on the second charge of voluntary manslaughter, leaving Snoop free and clear to pursue his career. He's since avoided mix-ups in violent crime, and has diversified his talents into films, more music, a clothing line, the *Girls Gone Wild* series and, most recently, spokesman with Lee Iaccoca for Chrysler cars.

Snoop and co-defendant, flanked by
attorneys David Kenner and Donald Re

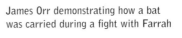
James Orr demonstrating how a bat
was carried during a fight with Farrah

Orr watches Fawcett's testimony
as judge Robert Altman listens

CAPTURED!

FARRAH FAWCETT
CHARLIE'S FALLEN ANGEL

People v. James Orr (1998)

Farrah demonstrates her version of how a bat was carried during a fight with Orr

L et me say this first: Farrah Fawcett is beautiful. Her famous mane of hair still frames a finely sculpted face, although age has added a few grays and lines. Her beauty is offset, however, by a sadness that stunned me.

The case started out with an odd, but sadly typical, domestic abuse moment: in February 1998, the police were summoned to writer-producer-director James Orr's Bel-Air home in response to a report of domestic violence. Fawcett and Orr's relationship was a tumultuous one—the previous year, Farrah had been accused by Orr's *other* girlfriend of stealing $75,000 in clothes and nude photos from Orr's house during a jealous rampage. According to the February police report, Farrah had turned down Orr's marriage proposal, a conflict escalated, and the former Charlie's Angel took her stuff and fled the

house. She alleged that Orr followed her out, grabbed her throat, threw her to the ground, and kicked her. At the time, Farrah said the incident was greatly exaggerated, and asked the L.A.P.D. to drop the case.

But they didn't, and instead pursued charges of "battery in a dating relationship," which carried a fine of $12,000 and a two-year jail sentence. In August 1998, Farrah took the stand to testify that her former boyfriend knocked her to the ground and beat her head on the pavement of his driveway. Wearing a large cross, and whispering much of her testimony, Farrah appeared ethereal, her gaunt face made smaller by the blonde hair that whirled around it. She seemed confused and shaken. Her frailty gave me the impression that she was a terribly insecure woman.

When the defense questioned her,

Farrah Fawcett describing her injuries

the case took an interesting turn. Farrah admitted that she had smashed the windows of his home with a fireplace poker and attacked his car with a baseball bat prior to the driveway beating. She said she carried the bat to defend herself; Orr said she yanked and pulled at his hair, and was an "insanely jealous woman." Watching the case was like watching performance art: Farrah demonstrated how she walked with the bat pointed down, at her side; Orr showed how she swung it as she walked. Orr demonstrated how he protected himself against her swinging arms, and a lawyer remarked that the whole thing looked like a bad dance.

THE VERDICT

Guilty. Orr's sentence: three years of summary probation, 100 hours of community service, 104 hours of batterer's counseling, a fine of $500 to be donated to a domestic violence fund, and an order to cease any and all contact with Farrah.

The courtroom seemed split down the middle. Her fans sympathized with her apparent vulnerability; his sympathizers identified with being allegedly stalked and attacked by a jealous ex-lover. I found fault with both parties, but my heart went out to the gorgeous Charlie's Angel.

Heidi Fleiss in federal-issue prison uniform, initially laughing at her situation

Attorney Donald Marks asking for bail for his client

HEIDI FLEISS
PEEKING INTO
THE LITTLE BLACK BOOK

United States Government v. Heidi Fleiss (1996)

Fleiss breaks down at the counsel table when reality hits

A true capitalist, Heidi Fleiss sold anything and everything to get money, and did the same to keep her income from the government. Of course, that might be because her trade was sex—not exactly legal to begin with. Not that that prevented her from raking in the cash.

"Hollywood Madam" Heidi Fleiss was 30 years old when her "girls" quite literally had Los Angeles by the tail. Federal prosecutors accused her of laundering $300,000 through her family's bank accounts, a conspiracy involving her father, pediatrician-to-the-stars Paul Fleiss. Her escorts made at least $2,500 a night, and while they were never prosecuted, Fleiss's unclaimed 40% of the take landed her in front of an L.A. judge in 1997.

During the trial, I felt trapped in a soap opera casting call. Lawyers, tourists, and even federal marshals packed the courtroom to get an eyeful of some of the tearful witnesses, all beautiful call girls. Heidi herself started the trial in high spirits, wisecracking, smirking, winking, and smiling; she seemed to believe she had all the power in the room. As the days wore on, though, the confident madam turned into a bedraggled prisoner, her oversized prison-issue uniform dwarfing her. Reality was setting in for the young woman, and it wasn't pretty.

Even more surreal than her transformation, even more surreal than her groupies in "Free Heidi" bomber jackets and testimonies about high-flying, high-paying johns, was Charlie Sheen's testimony. The circumstances were as L.A. as L.A. gets: he wanted to avoid the spectacle and was working, he said, and so he *sent a videotape of his testimony.* I don't know of any other town that would let a federal witness get away with that arrangement—any other courtroom would've slapped Sheen with contempt faster than he could say "I paid for sex." He *did* pay for sex, of course—the actor admitted to spending more than $50,000 in 1995 on Heidi's girls. In the end, I sketched Sheen's videotaped testimony, creating an image of an image.

Sheen's televised face only whetted the public's interest. Who were her other clients? What other blockbuster stars paid for prostitutes? How much did they pay? Heidi's "little black book" soon became the hottest property in Hollywood, and all of us waited for the moment when the prosecution would release its secrets.

THE VERDICT

Guilty. Fleiss was sentenced to thirty-seven months in a federal prison, 300 hours of community services, and a whopping $400 fine. She had learned her lesson, she told the judge, who seemed to believe her when she said, "I believe you will be a positive role model for other young people and other women who could benefit from the experiences you've had."

Twenty-one months later, Fleiss was out on good behavior. She owns a lingerie boutique on Hollywood Boulevard

Heidi making an appearance in her "jailhouse blues" in front of Judge Consuelo B. Marshall

Financial records are revealed

Fleiss's brother, mother, and father flank attorneys while she listens to the judge

called—what else?—Hollywood Madam. Her autobiography, *Pandering*, is available there, as well, and sometime in the future, we'll all get to see Heidi on the silver screen—or maybe a version of her played by Nicole Kidman, anyway. We've already seen her on the small screen, with *The Sopranos*'s Jamie-Lynn DiScala starring in *Call Me: The Rise and Fall of Heidi Fleiss.* Seven years ago, Fleiss told a federal judge that she was "young and stupid and . . . wrong," for launching her call-girl ring, but it looks like she's found a savvy way to make legal cash out of her illegal activities. She is now planning a "stud farm" in Nevada, where those activities are legal.

In the end, the public's own thirst for lust was never satiated: the contents of her "little black book" have never been released. Other than Charlie Sheen's televised admission of guilt, we might never know who else sinned with one of Heidi's girls.

Charlie Sheen testifies on video in federal court

CAPTURED!

MEL GIBSON
THE PASSION OF THE STALKER

Mel Gibson v. Zack Sinclair (2005)

Mel Gibson reads from rambling letters
sent to him by Zack Sinclair

When Mel Gibson made *The Passion of the Christ,* he hoped he would inspire a few fans to go to church. However, I'm not so sure that he thought he would inspire anyone to move in down the street and go to his church. But being that he's Mel Gibson and this is Los Angeles, that's exactly what happened.

Here's the story: Zack Sinclair, a 34-year-old Idahoan with a history of mental instability, saw *The Passion* and sent Gibson a few fan letters. And a few more. And more. Mostly he wanted to pray with Gibson, and have a conversation about their faith. When his letters didn't result in a meeting of souls, Sinclair moved into a boarding house in Malibu. One day, he went to Gibson's home, knocked at the door, and was told Gibson didn't live there. I guess bearing false witness isn't a sin if you're the hired help.

Patience is a virtue, though, and Sinclair sat on Gibson's wall and waited that day. Eventually, he went to Gibson's church to *demand* prayer time; soon after, Gibson sent him a commandment in the form of a restraining order. He visited Gibson's house again, and was arrested.

Sinclair, who had already proven himself to be a few cardinals short of a conclave, decided to defend himself in court. He was as mild-mannered as a banker and as cute as an altar boy, and his parents, who came to trial every day, were smiling and laughing, dressed in khakis like they planned to go to Disneyland every afternoon. For all I know, they did.

Perry Mason, he's not. But he was at least smart enough to ensure he would get to face Mel Gibson in person—once Gibson took the stand, as defense attorney, Sinclair would have an opportunity to fire questions at will. And he would do

Malibu Sheriff Winn testifying about arresting Zack Sinclair

had blown away terrorists and diplomats and soldiers and swarms of raiding Britons? He was on a movie screen somewhere else. Mel Gibson hadn't come to this courtroom. This guy was just Mel.

He took the stand and read letters Sinclair had sent to him—eventually, he asked if he had to read every one. While Sinclair wasn't particularly "scary or overtly threatening," Gibson did comment that, "This young man doesn't appear to know his boundaries," which was what concerned the actor. The stalker stared at him the entire time, and as the judge offered him the chance to examine the witness, we all thought, "*You've got him.*" Sinclair, the man who had gone to jail to meet Mel Gibson, now had an opportunity to ask him anything he wanted, plumb the depths of his psyche, really dig into the man himself.

"Any questions from the defense?"

"No, your honor."

He didn't even ask one question. That, to me, showed how disturbed he was. Why spend all this time and energy chasing the golden goose, only to ignore it when it's presented to you on a platter?

it in a roomful of swooning women.

Braveheart was scheduled to testify at 11:00 A.M. By 10:15, the room was packed with a collection of freshly lipsticked, breathless court reporters, lawyers, journalists, and assistants—every woman in the building had piled in to get a glimpse. It was Mel Gibson, after all! The guy whose butt had caused millions of

women to press pause during *Lethal Weapon,* whose disarming grin and intense sense of vengeance had fueled a dozen or so blockbusters. One young district attorney told me outright: "I'm so hot right now. I'm in love with Mel Gibson!"

Cameras weren't allowed in the courtroom, but the judge hadn't written a contingency plan for millennial technolo-

gy. In the courtroom and on the other side of the entry's glass doors, dozens of camera phones waited at the ready for the moment when Mel Gibson himself would take the stand.

And take the stand he did. All scruffy-bearded, annoyed-at-the-stalker 5'9" of him. Oh, he's a nice-looking guy, to be sure, but his persona, the man who

Here's the prosecutor, treating the proceedings like it's a real case, presenting evidence, asking questions, making arguments, and Sinclair just kicked back in his nice suit at his table, silent as a church mouse.

Gibson descended from the stand and left as soon as he could, accompanied by the two luckiest sheriffs in the county. Now, I suppose, is a good time to let you know that the sheriffs in L.A. are no different than any other Angelenos—they like walking with the stars. They like being in the pictures. In the world of celebrity trials, they're celebrities themselves, and they love it.

THE VERDICT

Guilty of felony stalking. The sentence? Sinclair had to undergo three months of psychiatric evaluation before a punishment was determined in June, 2005. He acted as his own attorney during the sentencing as well, and was sentenced to three years in prison, where, one presumes, he'll have plenty of time to pray.

Darlene Gillespie at her federal trial, with a fraudulent check projected behind her

DARLENE GILLESPIE
M-I-C . . . SEE YOU IN PRISON!

United States Government v. Darlene Gillespie (1999)

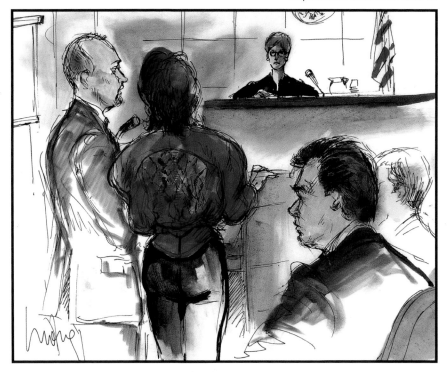

Attorney Charles Rondeau with his client,
as prosecutor Jack Weiss looks on

M—I—C . . . See you in prison! K- E - Y . . . Why? Because you're a felon!

Such was the song that was on the day Darlene Gillespie showed up in court to fight charges that she had committed conspiracy, securities fraud, mail fraud, obstruction of justice, perjury . . . a total of 26 counts adding up to s-t-e-a-l-i-n-g. Only months after the former Mouseketeer was sentenced to three months of probation for attempting to return a stolen food processor to a department store, she was indicted for lying under oath to the Securities and Exchange Commission—and committing several counts of fraud on top of that.

Using overdrawn and closed accounts, she and her fiancé, Jerry Fraschilla, purchased large amounts of stock and began earning profits. In 1995, the SEC resolved a suit with them and they had to pay a fine, but that wasn't enough for the Feds. Believing the couple lied, fabricated evidence, produced false documents and used a fictitious name for the transactions, the Feds decided to quite literally make a federal case out of it.

I dress differently depending on where the case is—for Beverly Hills, for instance, I'll go designer, but I'll dress down a bit if I'm attending court downtown. But with federal cases, it's conservative all the way. With so much protocol and formality, it's traditional to dress conservatively, as though attending a board meeting.

Darlene Gillespie's sartorial choices, however, were not particularly traditional. She's very, very tiny—Mouseketeer-tiny—and her fiery red,

Prosecutor Jack Weiss discussing
bad checks (in background)

THE VERDICT

Guilty. Guilty, guilty, guilty, twelve times over. Darlene Fraschilla was sentenced to two years in a federal prison for her scheming. (She had married Jerry two months before her sentencing, and was sentenced under her married name.)

One thing I realized during this case: you never outgrow your mouse ears. Every shred of publicity about the trial mentioned her Disney days, and even now, if you go online, it's easier to find her smiling face framed by braids and mouse ears than it is to find a recent picture. I hope she and Jerry are living a fraud-free, mouse-free life these days.

bouffant-and-shag hair would've been better suited for a diner in the 1950s than on a 56-year-old woman in 1999. She wore a leather jacket with red and pink reptile-skin inserts, black stretch pants, ultra-high heels, and metallic nail polish on her long fingernails. To her credit, she did occasionally show up in a tweed suit—but always paired with an eye-wateringly bright floral blouse. She looked nothing like a Mouseketeer, and every bit the hardened moll of a professional thief. And there was no doubt that she was that; her fiancé Fraschilla had pleaded guilty to 21 counts of fraud, and was sentenced to 18 months in prison.

Soon Ja Du

Soon Ja Du cries while viewing security videotape of Latasha Harlins entering her convenience store

Witness describing Latasha Harlins's movements in Soon Ja Du's convenience store

Witness describing Latasha Harlins's movements in Soon Ja Du's convenience store

LATASHA HARLINS
STOKING THE FIRES OF UNREST

People v. Soon Ja Du (1991)

Less than two weeks after the beating of Rodney King became the most-watched reality show in primetime, 15-year-old Latasha Harlins walked into Empire Liquor in downtown Los Angeles and slipped a bottle of orange juice into her backpack. Whether she planned to pay for it is a matter of conjecture, but the events that followed were caught on security camera: Soon Ja Du, the wife of the store's owner, accuses her of stealing; she tugs on Latasha's shirt; Latasha punches Soon in the face four times; Soon throws a chair at her; Latasha turns to walk away and Soon shoots her in the back of the head, killing her.

The shooting was tragic enough, but to happen within weeks of Rodney King? That bullet was like throwing a truck full of napalm onto a raging inferno. Ice Cube wrote a song called "Black Korea," a diatribe against Korean delis;

Empire Liquor was firebombed.

I attended the trial against Soon Ja Du, and one look at the woman convinced me that she was devastated. I don't think she meant to kill Harlins; working at a store that had 40 shoplifting incidents a week, and a history of 30 burglaries, probably put her on edge. But that hardly mattered to Harlins's family.

The trial itself was entertaining—colorful and dramatic witnesses, interesting and sad circumstances, and lawyers that knew how to put on a good show.

THE VERDICT

Guilty of voluntary manslaughter. On November 15, 1995, Soon Ja Du was sentenced to five years of probation, 400 hours of community service, and fines—an unusually light sentence, and one that hardly satisfied the black community's sense of justice.

Soon Ja Du listens with headphones to testimony during her trial

Dustin Hoffman takes the stand, and shows the video package from his film, *Tootsie*

DUSTIN HOFFMAN
TOOT, TOOT, TOOTSIE, GOODBYE

Dustin Hoffman v. Los Angeles Magazine (1999)

I work in fashion as well as courtrooms; I know the business can be a tough one. Every so often, a model's photograph is altered—either with an airbrush or with a whole new body. It happens. But the Dustin Hoffman case was the first time I ever knew of a man complaining about it—make that a man who was dressed as a woman.

We all loved *Tootsie*, both the movie and the "woman." It won Dustin Hoffman an Oscar nomination and brought cross-dressing to a new level. *Los Angeles Magazine* loved Tootsie, too—so much so that they superimposed her head onto the body of a model wearing a butter-colored silk gown. The issue was called "Fabulous Hollywood," and they gave the same updated-fashion treatment to stars ranging from Cary Grant to Grace Kelly. Dustin Hoffman didn't find the

shoot as amusing as some did; he figured if he had actually agreed to dress up as Tootsie and model the gown himself, he would have been paid millions of dollars. He sued under the Lanham Act, which prohibits the use of a celebrity's identity for an unauthorized commercial endorsement. The magazine said it wasn't an advertisement, but an editorial piece, and they were covered under the First Amendment.

In his semi-crew-cut, Hoffman might have looked a bit silly, but he was all business. He took copious notes, remained serious, and emanated that low-grade, slow-burn intensity that's served his career so well. The courtroom was packed to capacity; apparently, everyone wanted to see the great actor in an unscripted performance.

THE VERDICT

Guilty . . . and then not guilty. The first trial found in favor of Hoffman, saying he had been "violated by technology," a phrase I find to be both amusing and a lit-

tle creepy. In July 2001, though, a federal appeals court overturned the $3 million judgment, stating the photo spread was not an advertisement, and was protected under the First Amendment.

Hoffman takes copious notes during the federal court proceedings

JOE HUNT
THE BILLIONAIRE BOYS CLUB

People v. Joe Hunt (1987)

Rarely does a murder plot brilliantly capture a decade's zeitgeist, but Joe Hunt of the Billionaire Boys Club was someone special. He was the kind of wunderkind that typified the spirit of the 1980s—he was driven by power and money, flashy cars and big houses, and no one and nothing would get in his way.

The world was changing; the stock market was booming, deregulation had enormous conglomerates growing more enormous by the second, and people who normally never heard a word about stocks suddenly knew about junk bonds, trading, and investments. Lamborghinis, DeLoreans, *Lifestyles of the Rich and Famous*—everywhere America looked, there was more evidence of the fabulous lives other people lived. Joe Hunt, a young investment genius determined to grab the brass ring, developed a number of scams, and none of them were straightforward; like most "big cons," his plans took forethought, planning, and the cooperation of often unwitting accomplices. Those accomplices were the young men of the Billionaire Boys Club (BBC), an investment club he founded.

The "boys" of the BBC loved their lives in Beverly Hills, and were wildly successful at bringing in investors. Hunt's interview was a bit unusual; he asked the prospective boys if they'd ever commit murder. Then he would ask if they'd commit murder to save their mothers. "Then you can't claim that you have a line you won't cross," he said.

Hunt was extraordinarily eloquent and charming, and he had several philosophies of business and investing that he freely shared with his prospective investors and boys. His favorite was the "paradox" philosophy, which boiled down to: Not only is everything relative, but the ends justify the means. In the money business that can lead one into some sticky ethical situations; in the business of life, that can lead to murder.

And it did—twice. The first victim, Ron Levin, met with Hunt to discuss his investments. He saw through the young man immediately, recognizing that Hunt wasn't investing any money, just pouring it into the BBC boys; he laughed at their gullibility. He did agree to allow Hunt to test his mettle, and set up a $5 million credit line through the BBC. Hunt could invest it, and the BBC would get to keep half of the profits. Less than two months later, Hunt nearly tripled the credit line; Levin closed the account.

But then Levin disappeared. After a quick investigation, Hunt found out the transaction had never been supported by any money; he'd been conned. Ego bruised, and broke, Hunt hired a bodyguard. He made a list. They broke into Levin's apartment, forced him to sign a check from a Swiss bank account for $1.5 million, and shot him. Then they drove his body to Soledad Canyon in Los Angeles, shot his face a few more times to make it unrecognizable, and left it there.

Despite his planning, though, Hunt realized he'd left the contract, correspondence, and even his "to-do" list at Levin's house. Even worse, when he tried to cash the check, the check was refused. Hunt gathered together his boys and described the crime to them. The boys began feeling uneasy about Hunt and their involvement in the BBC, and some began taking notes for the police.

Enter his next scheme, which revolved solely around the death of a BBC boy's father. The boys would kidnap Hedayat Eslaminia, force him to sign his wealth over to his son, and upon his death, his son, Reza, would invest the business into the BBC. During the kidnapping, they stuffed the man into a trunk; after a few hours, they re-opened the trunk to find Eslaminia, dead. They dumped the body in the canyon. Once again, though, they found that the payoff wasn't nearly as generous as they'd hoped.

Hunt began planning more murders, but before he could carry them out, he was arrested. His fingerprints matched the to-do list. Hunt hired an attorney and, finally, Dean Karny, a trusted member of the BBC, went to the police and asked for immunity in exchange for full disclosure. A few weeks later, a dead man was found in a hotel with a credit card slip bearing Karny's name—but Karny had an alibi,

and other BBC members remembered Hunt mentioning such a scheme. (That murder remains unsolved.)

At long last, I entered the picture. There were two trials, one for each murder, and in his first few appearances, Hunt swaggered in, smug and cocky. But like so many other arrogant defendants, time in jail humbled him. By the second trial, his hair had been cut close, and he'd become very thin in his jail jumpsuit. No matter how invincible you feel, spending months in jail is enough to remind anyone that they're powerless.

The most disturbing thing, to me, was his general attitude during the trial. I think the answer to "why" is even simpler than for money—it's "Why the hell not?" He believed he could do it, and he did. But he didn't get away with it.

THE VERDICT

Guilty of murdering Ron Levin with special circumstances. In the 1992 trial for Eslaminia's death, the jury deadlocked, and charges were dropped. No matter, though—Hunt had life in prison without parole for the murder of Levin, so one more life sentence wasn't likely to punish him further. After finding an error in their trial, the courts reviewed the kidnapping and murder convictions of Reza Eslaminia and Ben Dosti. Ben's conviction was dropped to voluntary manslaughter and kidnapping, and he was freed from prison in 1998. Reza's case was thrown out in 2000, and he, too, is free. Dean Karny has a new identity under the Witness Protection Program, and after passing the California Bar, is presumably practicing law somewhere in California.

The story has a strange epilogue, which I cover in more detail later on in the book. A juicy, glamorous story like this couldn't be passed up by the television networks, and Brat Packer Judd Nelson starred in the *Billionaire Boys Club,* a 1989 TV movie that told the tale of Joe Hunt. At home in Beverly Hills, two young brothers were enraptured by Hunt's plans, sure they could escape his unfortunate ending. Two months later, on August 20, 1989, Lyle and Eric Menendez shot their parents in hopes of fulfilling the get-rich quick dream of the Billionaire Boys Club.

1996
ABC NEWS

MICHAEL
JACKSON
"JACKSON
FAMILY
HONORS"
FEDERAL TRIAL

MICHAEL JACKSON PLAYING PEEK-A-BOO

Smith-Hemion Productions v. MJJ Productions, Inc. Michael Jackson et al. (1996)

Michael Jackson stifles a giggle during his federal trial

Once the King of Pop, Michael Jackson might also go down in history as the King of Weird. The fresh-faced boy who wowed critics and audiences with *Off the Wall* in 1979 became the performer of the best-selling album of all time in 1982 with *Thriller*. The world happily wrapped itself around his rhinestone-gloved pinky.

Then the weirdness began.

The plastic surgeries made him into a poster boy for *Extreme Makeover*. His ranch, Neverland, was home to a personal zoo of exotic animals. He wore a filter mask in public. He seemed to publicly betray a close friend, Paul McCartney, when he bought out The Beatles's songbook. Then boys came forward with dis-

A portrait of the "king of pop," 1996, federal court, L.A.

turbing stories. Yet it wasn't the boys in his bed that were the subject of the first Jackson lawsuit I witnessed—fraud was.

Suits and countersuits seemed to blossom under the moonwalker's feet. He was suing *Hard Copy* for $100 million for slander and, at the same time, he was being sued by Neverland Ranch employees and the two boys who alleged that he molested them. Meanwhile, I was working on a case involving the 1994 television special *Jackson Family Honors,* an unsuccessful show. Instead of giving a solo performance as promised, Michael handed out two awards and sang a song with his family.

I've been in a lot of circus-like courtrooms, but I think Jackson takes the prize for "Best Sideshow Act." Lobster Boy has nothing on this guy. He dressed in his usual red shirt, white undershirt, white socks, and slim black trousers—I

can't imagine how many sets of that getup fill the closets at Neverland—with mirrored glasses tucked into his pocket. Jet-black hair fell in gentle tendrils around his blue-white face. As if his appearance weren't jarring enough, his antics crossed the line into surreal: on the witness stand, he giggled at us, waved, and, at one point, he covered his face in such a way that I'd swear he was playing peek-a-boo.

THE VERDICT

Plaintiff wins. By September 1996, the jury awarded Smith-Hemion Productions $2.6 million after finding that they had been defrauded. Bizarrely, they couldn't decide which members of the Jackson family should pay up, and how much, and expressed confusion over the judge's instructions. The judge told lawyers to prepare for a mistrial. In that case, at least, Jackson was off the hook.

Since then, he's dangled his baby over a balcony, filed for bankruptcy, and been the object of yet another high-profile trial (see next chapter). The one thing that *has* remained consistent is Jackson's ability to capture the headlines and his fondness for red shirts.

Joe Jackson testifying in federal court during the Jackson Family Honors case

SMITH-HEMION PRODUCTIONS V. MJJ PRODUCTIONS, INC. MICHAEL JACKSON ET AL.

83

MICHAEL JACKSON
NEVERLAND'S LOST BOY

People v. Michael Jackson (2005)

A portrait of the "king of pop,"
2005, superior court, Santa Maria

Last year, I walked into a coffee shop to grab my hit of morning caffeine and choked—within a few months, the price of the cup had gone up no less than 150%, from one dollar to $2.50. The little shop, which had once sold doughnuts and grilled cheese sandwiches, now had a menu full of ingredients like arugula and avocado. Later that week, the local government charged a cool grand for an "impact fee": I had dared to set up my easel in the parking lot of the courthouse, which apparently creates a thousand dollars' worth of impact on the asphalt. Elsewhere in the parking lot, two surfer girls pushed baby buggies around, hawking the books that lay nestled cozily inside. Business boomed everywhere in this community located within California's bucolic Central Coast region.

Michael Jackson had come to town.

I'm sure you've heard the whole tale, but in a nutshell: ten years after Michael Jackson settled out-of-court with 13-year-old Jordy Chandler's family, Jackson retained criminal attorneys to defend him against similar charges. Within a month, Jackson appeared on the BBC, saying it's A-OK to sleep with young boys in his bed while walking around Neverland with the two boys who would be featured in the case. Fearing media exposure, the trial was moved to little Santa Maria, California, bringing with it the carnival: the media stood barking for more customers, and the freak show of Jackson's fans entertained the world.

A lawn bowling green is right next to the courthouse, and every day ancient old men rolled their red and blue balls down the green, doing their best to ignore the satellite trucks all around them. Each day, a woman drove her daughters to the

Documentary filmmaker Martin Bashir
watches video, *Living with Michael Jackson,*
as Jackson covers his face and cries

courthouse just in time to see Jackson exit his car, the little girls shrieked and wailed at the sight of him, and the woman piled them back into the car and got to school just in time for homeroom. Another woman waved around a puppet of Michael Jackson; scores of his fans quit their jobs and maxed out their credit cards to stay in one of the nearby hotels.

The media stood like cattle in actual pens (Pen #1, Pen #2, etc.), and I occasionally wondered if bales of hay would make the situation more festive. Open-sided white tents had been hastily erected for the scads of journalists, letting in the coastal wind and the winter rains; my drawing board went flying across the parking lot on more than one occasion. (At least in the Simpson case we cattle had trailers.)

Come to think of it, we were more like veal than cattle. The judge was extraordinarily strict, and every hour and 45 minutes, we had a ten-minute break—just enough time to go to the bathroom or grab a snack and run back to the courtroom. After a few months, I noticed we all put on weight from sitting for seven hours a day, eating Power bars and the local pseudo-sandwiches. And there was no give on these breaks, none at all; a lawyer could be in the middle of a sentence, but the bailiff stood on cue, and the judge interrupted to announce the break. As though that strict regimen weren't enough, the most popular sheriff had a German shepherd named Zeus who only understood German. All the ladies loved the bomb-sniffing dog—he had a badge and everything—and I suspect that the other sheriffs were jealous from all the feminine attention he garnered.

After all the fun of the Robert Blake trial (and I enjoy murder trials more, anyway), Jackson's trial—the case itself, the circus around it, and the three-hour drive to Santa Maria—depressed me so much that I didn't attend on a daily basis. I only went for the most important witnesses, in my opinion: the accuser, his mother, and Jackson's former accusers and housekeepers—people who had something to offer to the case. I didn't attend for the celebrity witnesses; I had seen celebrities before. What I wanted to see was some version of the truth.

And the truth was, Michael Jackson is an appropriate leader for the devotees who surround him. He doesn't look like he's of this earth. He could be an extra-terrestrial.

You heard about the pajamas, dancing on the car, his repeated visits to the hospital, but seeing him every day just enhances the weird factor. His skin, so pale, appears to be peeling in places, and he never wiped his face or wiped his eyes; he only dabbed them, like a genteel lady conscious of smearing her makeup. His hair does *not* look real to me, and his habit of pushing it back from his face, carefully, with two hands—never smoothing it—contributed to that impression. That, and it would be different lengths on different days of the week. And occasionally, he would show up with a soul patch that I'd swear was penciled in.

His overdone, sparkly clothes contributed to the un-reality. Luftwaffe jackets with epaulets and rhinestone cufflinks; linen jackets with black satin pants; little gold charms dangled from a watch chain draped across his brocade vest. . . . He wore his watch on his right wrist and a Kabbalah bracelet on the left; his feet were clad in white socks and Huarachi sandals.

Being that I'm the fashion illustra-

"The Empty Chair"; waiting and watching the clock as Jackson is late for court

tor, everyone asked about his "motif"—was it a serpent motif on his armband? A dragon motif? A military or Chinese motif on the jacket? My answer? Captain Marvel. Here's a man with loads of money, who could dress as a dandy or a fop, Oscar Wilde-style, with brilliant antique cufflinks and velvet jackets, and it would work beautifully for him. Instead, he dresses like a twelve-year-old kid dressing up as the richest guy in the world. He looked like a version of Willy Wonka so weird even Tim Burton couldn't capture it on film—like a live-action cartoon.

And his *family*. They all showed up in their white "solidarity" outfits. His father has tattooed eyebrows and moustache, big gold earrings, and this man—who Michael supposedly detested, who supposedly made him into the alien creature he is today—walked into the courtroom with him every day, hand-in-hand,

nice as you please. Katherine, his mother, took notes in her little Louis Vuitton notebook; a few of his brothers showed up occasionally. Janet and LaToya came only on the first and last day, and the Jackson assemblage—a very black family surrounding this chalk-white ghost of a superstar—was unsettling, to say the least.

The most bizarre thing, though, is that *Michael Jackson never moved*. I'm very aware of body language. I use it in my drawings and watch closely for the moment when someone turns his head to shed a new angle on my work. But he's the stillest person I've ever drawn. He stared forward, hands on the table before

him, back rigid, and held perfectly still for hours at a time. I even tried to catch him blinking. When they showed the documentary that had triggered the accusations, he tapped his foot to his music; he cried a little when he saw himself talking about his childhood; and thereafter, sat still as a mannequin.

The faceless accuser details fondling by Jackson while on a private jet hired to fly group from Miami to California, while Jackson, wearing drawstring bottoms with palm trees, sobs into a tissue

If you haven't seen the documentary, you're missing out on one of the most disturbing pieces of video in recent history. Jackson's sitting there, trying to salvage a once-great career, talking about his own difficult childhood, and he sits hand-in-hand with a young cancer survivor whose head rests on his shoulder. The boy—the child in question—turned his head occasionally to gaze at Jackson, eyes wide and worshipful, like a girl on a first date. The interior of his house is similar to his clothes: a child's idea of royalty, rococo nudes of little children, six chandeliers in the living room, and thousands of gilt-edged books that I suspect the King of Pop has never cracked open.

At one point, the boy and his little brother shot their own video at Neverland; the younger boy wanted to be an actor, and he believed Jackson would help him in his career. They walked

PEOPLE V. MICHAEL JACKSON

The Jackson family in court

Prosecutor Ron Zonen questions accuser's faceless mother, breaking down on the stand, while Jackson smiles

around Neverland, Jackson (holding his ever-present black umbrella) wheeling around the older boy bald and weak from his radiation treatments. The narration, provided by the younger brother, questioned the necessity of the wheelchair. The boy could walk, he said on the stand, but Michael said to put him in the wheelchair.

The children's testimonies were the most difficult to hear. Jason Franzia, the boy in question in the 1993 case, was recently married; he had never told anyone the details of what had happened between him and Jackson. A religious young man who juggles his time between a car parts store and a position as a youth pastor, he clearly did *not* want to relive that particular chapter in his life. One bit of testimony I remember: he testified that Jackson gave him $100 for every time he could tickle Jason, and he burst into tears on the stand. My mouth dropped open, and as I looked around the courtroom, several women—who I knew to be mothers—were also stunned. The moms, it seemed, all believed him. The jury snickered.

Eventually, John Doe took the stand. This boy sat in front of a group of antagonists and described how a superstar had masturbated him to the point of ejaculation; again, the mother in me can't imagine any teenager who would want to put himself through that unless he told the truth. Maybe I don't want to believe he would lie about such a thing. But any truth in this case was diluted by one question that plagued us all: what mother in her right mind would allow her son to sleep in a bed with a man who had already been accused of molestation once?

One day, you may remember, Jackson didn't show up on time. At 8:31 A.M., the judge took the bench; at 8:35 A.M., he said he would give the defen-

dant one more minute to show before holding him in contempt. I, meanwhile, sketched furiously, capturing the judge and the empty seat as quickly as I could. The judge made another statement at 8:36 A.M., holding Jackson in contempt of court and giving him one hour to show up before he would be taken into custody.

My next sketch in the series is labeled 9:30 A.M.: Jackson strolls in and has a seat, clad in his pajamas.

The distorted sense of reality hit full bloom when defense attorney Thomas Mesereau dropped names like Elizabeth Taylor and Marlon Brando, as though Jackson's famous friends were proof of his

normalcy. Because, heaven knows, Elizabeth Taylor and Marlon Brando are just typical, normal folks like us.

THE VERDICT

Not guilty on all counts. I understood the verdict. No one came off well in this case. Either the mother was setting her son up to lie for money, truly believing a man who slept with boys was safe, or she was setting her son up to get molested in hopes of getting cash in the deal. Whether or not Jackson did it, it seems, is irrelevant. What's relevant is that this family somehow convinced themselves that getting attention and money from the King of Pop meant they were special.

And that's really what all of these fans are about—the woman with her two little girls, the woman who released doves for every acquittal, the mother who never once seemed to question why Michael Jackson was so interested in her son: the belief that "if that star really knew me, we'd be best friends. And we'd hang out, and he'd love me as much as I love him."

JEFFREY KATZENBERG
THE NOT-SO-HAPPIEST PLACE ON EARTH

Jeffrey Katzenberg v. Michael Eisner (1999)

Jeffrey Katzenberg and wife
watch Michael Eisner's testimony

In what was probably the most exclusive trial of my career, I watched two of the most powerful, wealthy men in Hollywood resort to name-calling and backbiting. I guess maybe all men really are little boys on the inside?

Jeffrey Katzenberg, former studio boss of Disney, resigned from the company in 1994 to start the DreamWorks SKG studio with Steven Spielberg and David Geffen. After leaving, though, he claimed he hadn't received several bonuses he was owed from the company—bonuses that totaled somewhere in the range of $250 million. I think I'd be irked if someone cheated me out of that much dough, too. Michael Eisner, chairman of Disney, claimed that the bonuses were dependent upon Katzenberg's performance, and that his movies hadn't earned enough to award him the bonuses. It seemed an odd suggestion, especially since the studio had churned out *Pretty Woman, Aladdin,* and Academy-Award-winning *Beauty and the Beast* during Katzenberg's tenure. Eisner also said he hated the "little midget," which could indicate why Katzenberg believed the bonuses were withheld for personal reasons.

I had never been in a case like this one, and, I'm sad to say, probably won't witness another. The trial was private, in posh law offices, no jury, just a privately hired judge, and high security measures to protect the moguls. The press room even provided catered food—pastries, sandwiches, etc.—that was far from the vending-machine fare we're used to. The men were clearly busy—Eisner showed up once in a suit that still bore tailoring stitches—and they clearly despised each other. They had been friends when they worked together, but all that went out the window when Katzenberg defected.

Bert Fields showing the Arthur the Aardvark doll to the delight of the judge

Attorneys discussing finances of Katzenberg

Palpable hatred seethed from both of them.

The trial took on more than a few surreal moments. Disney's history of children's films meant that one attorney pulled out a stuffed Arthur the Aardvark and waved him around. Eisner admitted to calling Katzenberg a midget; in his defense, Katzenberg is not a large man. He's very kind, though—Katzenberg wrote me a letter saying he liked my drawings, and that it was a pleasure seeing my artwork in court. Flattery will you get you everywhere.

Attorney Bert Fields
questioning Michael Eisner

THE VERDICT

Out-of-court settlement. On July 7, 1999, the pair settled out of court, a foregone conclusion as far as I could tell. The terms of the deal were not disclosed, although both sides, naturally, said they were pleased to come to a mutually acceptable settlement. Since then, Katzenberg's had some great successes with DreamWorks. In 2001, *Shrek* was an enormous success that won the first Best Animated Picture Academy Award. Eisner released a memoir of his summer camp days, entitled *Camp*, and subsequently stepped down as chairman of Disney.

SANTÉ KIMES
NO BODY, NO CRIME

People v. Santé Kimes (2004)

I know a lot of people who claim to be bi-coastal—citizens of New York and L.A.—but I don't know any of them whose L.A. murder trial was delayed by their New York trial. The Kimeses are special people, though.

Think Bonnie and Clyde, with a few differences. Instead of robbing banks, they kited checks and set up insurance scams. Instead of gunning down bystanders and leaving them for dead, they shot a few select people and hid the bodies. Oh, and Santé and Kenneth are mother and son.

Read closely, or you might lose the trail of breadcrumbs. In December, 1997, Santé took out a hefty loan on a home in Las Vegas (where she had been convicted of enslaving Mexican aliens in 1986). Her secretary allegedly forged and notarized another friend's name, Dennis Kazdin, to the application. A few days after she

transferred ownership of the property to a homeless man who worked for her (and made him apply for an even bigger home-owner's insurance policy), the house burned to the ground.

Meanwhile, Kazdin received a payment booklet from the bank, a helpful reminder to pay his $280,000 loan. He complained; Santé tried to coax him into the scheme; he declined. Two months later, on March 13, 1998, Sean Little, a drifter, accompanied Kenneth Kimes to Kazdin's home and waited as Kenneth shot the man. They searched the house for any evidence linking Kazdin to the scheme, wrapped the body in bags, stuffed it in Kazdin's Jaguar, dumped the body in a dumpster at LAX, and bought a $100 bouquet of flowers for Santé. Kenneth loves his mother.

Three months later, the Kimeses took Manhattan, leaving a trail of bad

checks and arrest warrants behind them. Kenneth rented a $6,000 Upper East Side apartment from elderly Irene Silverman, who disappeared less than a month later. Authorities caught up with the grifters the same day, finding two guns, real estate transfer papers, blank social security cards, handcuffs, and $30,000 in cash in their Lincoln. They also found a note-book filled with Silverman's signature—

had Santé been practicing?

Silverman's body was never found, but in 2000, a New York jury convicted both Santé and Kenneth of murder. Santé got 120 years; Kenneth got 125. Throughout the trial, Kenneth wouldn't say boo about his mother, and in 2001, he held a Court TV reporter hostage with a pen to prevent his mother's impending extradition to California.

It didn't work. The pair were placed on a flight to Los Angeles to stand trial for Kazdin's murder.

Things changed in L.A.. Faced with the death penalty, Kenneth apparently decided he wanted to live out the full 125 years of his East Coast sentence—and whatever they had to give him in the West. He pleaded guilty and testified against his mother.

Their relationship, in a nutshell, was creepy. Santé had allegedly been sexually abused, so it seemed entirely possible that she had, in turn, abused Kenneth, exacting incredible control over his life. As if his testifying against her wasn't surprising enough, he also testified that the pair had killed a banker in the Bahamas in 1996. He also admitted to strangling Silverman and dumping her in a trash bin.

Santé wept as she sat in her wheelchair, clearly trying to get her son's sympathy, but to Kenneth's credit, he stayed strong. Perhaps the prospect of his own death was enough to break the ties forged by his mother. He refused to look at her, and cried his head off as he damned his mother to prison. He looked like a Harley-riding, old hippie kind of guy, with a long moustache, and a long, pretty braid of hair—kind of like an Edwardian

Santé Kimes in tears on the stand
(bandages from IVs are from her
frequent visits to the jail hospital)

fop who grew up in California. Two things really stuck with me about his testimony: he bought flowers for her on the way home from murdering a family friend; and apparently, every time he killed someone for her, Santé congratulated him. She also had a family motto: "No body, no crime." (Santé later said the family motto was "rainbows.")

Santé, herself, was a complete trip on the stand. She showed pictures of how beautiful she was, how rich she used to be, how she was married to a wealthy man, had estates and connections to the Republican party; she said she even went to the White House. Since it certainly didn't garner any sympathy from the jurors, her goal seemed to be to prove that she didn't need the money from the con games.

THE VERDICT

Guilty. Wonder of wonders, the jury believed Kenneth, not Santé. Kenneth knew he would be getting life in prison without parole; now his mother joined him. While he's serving his sentence in California, Santé returned to New York to serve her 120-year-sentence there. I think it's safe to say her hold on her son can't survive 3,000 miles and over a century in prison.

RODNEY KING
L.A. BURNS

United States of America v. Stacey C. Koon et al. (1993)

George Holliday shows the videotape he shot
of police beating in Rodney King trial

While I was not present at the original Rodney King trial, I remember it well. I live in Los Angeles, after all. The entire course of the trial was painful to live through, but after the acquittal in whitebread Simi Valley—a decision that stunned most of the country—the world changed for a few days.

Just as a refresher: on March 3, 1991, Rodney King was pulled over for driving recklessly after he refused to stop for the police. He reacted violently to police officers, and when tasers failed to subdue him, four officers spent the next few minutes beating him with batons—striking him a total of 56 times—until the man no longer tried to get up from the ground.

Unbeknownst to the participants, an on-looker named George Holliday was nearby with a handicam, filming what

would become the most-watched home video since Abraham Zapruder caught J.F.K.'s assassination on tape. The videotape seemed to capture all that was corrupt and wrong with the L.A.P.D., all the rage and defeat, and sent the entire country into a tailspin. When a young girl was killed by a Korean grocer (a case found elsewhere in this book), the racial tensions intensified. When a judge deemed Los Angeles to be biased, the trial of the four officers in question was sent to suburban Simi Valley. What appeared to be a racially-motivated beating would be tried by 10 whites, one Hispanic, and one Asian person.

Which brings us to April 29, 1992.

I was listening to the radio when I heard about the fires in South Central. People opined that South Central would

rise up and more or less invade Beverly Hills and Century City, bringing destruction and fire in its wake; I didn't know what to believe. I was about to attend a big dinner party, which seemed so distant from the violence in my own city that I couldn't quite make the reality connection. The city instituted martial law, meaning that the police and the National Guard were in control—pretty ironic when one considers the Rodney King case. My neighbors and I crowded into the street, and one of my neighbors, who had been in the Israeli army, told me not to worry. He had an Uzi, he said. Yippee, I thought.

We drove up to Mulholland Drive, the famous road that winds on top of the hills and offers a view of all of Los Angeles, and we saw dozens of bright orange lights, burning in the distance, scattered across the city. It looked oddly

Officer Tim Wind shows swings with a baton

Rodney King listens to witnesses

beautiful, almost like an encampment of Native Americans or Civil War soldiers, burning fires to keep away the night. Then we returned home; we had to get off of the streets before curfew.

Within the next five days, 54 people would die, 7,000 people would be arrested, and looting and fires resulted in over a billion dollars in damage. One of the victims was Reginald Denny, the truck driver who was pulled from his truck, beaten savagely, and who lay bleeding while his assailant did a victory dance over his body. The entire event, of course, was caught on tape. Damien "Football" Williams, the man who threw the slab of concrete that shattered Denny's head, was later acquitted of attempted murder and found guilty of one felony count of simple mayhem and one misdemeanor assault charge for Williams; he was sentenced to ten years in jail. Henry Watson, another assailant, was found guilty of one misdemeanor assault charge and given credit for time served.

A year later, I sketched the federal trial. After the acquittal and ensuing riots, President Bush himself announced that there would be a federal investigation to decide if the beating was in violation of the 14th Amendment—in other words,

motivated by race. Instead of Simi Valley, this trial occurred in the Roybal Building, the new federal courthouse in L.A.; it seemed appropriate that this case would christen the courtroom. The building was so new, in fact, that we weren't permitted to set drawing boards on the benches because they could scratch the teak.

Fronting the courthouse was a huge sculpture of a figure shot through with holes, nicknamed "Drive By."

We were the only case in the entire courthouse, and the only food source was a cafeteria owned by Host International, so we all went to Little Tokyo or Chinatown for lunch. It was the year the

Los Angeles Metro opened, and we took the novel form of transportation—not a car! A train!—to lunch every day. Then we would return to the big building that was more crowded on the outside than in.

Black activists showed up every day to demonstrate, and as the trial wore on, the police presence grew stronger and stronger. Inside, the trial affected me in ways I didn't expect. I sympathized with Rodney King, but with the officers, too. King was beaten terribly, but the police pursued him in an eight-mile chase before he pulled over; he charged them, and not even 50,000 volts of electricity stopped him from fighting them. The boys in blue aren't supposed to lose control of their emotions, but this time they did, and it was caught on tape.

As the jury filed out to begin deliberating, the entire city tiptoed around on eggshells. Would there be another riot? Guilty or not guilty? One juror allegedly went to the top floor of the courthouse every day to report, "Well, South Central isn't burning yet." The police told the media they would issue bulletproof vests if we wanted them, fearing for our lives as we walked from the car to the courtroom. Most of us declined. Deliberations went on for two weeks, and "verdict watch" became something of a slumber party. We gossiped, played Trivial Pursuit, and I even set up a makeshift bowling alley in the courthouse hallway. We had no idea when the jury would resurface, but we all knew we had to be there when it happened.

THE VERDICT

Guilty. On Easter Sunday, 1993, the jury pronounced Stacey Koon and Laurence Powell guilty of violating King's civil rights. The other officers, Tim Wind and Theodore Briseno, were found not guilty. No riots ensued. On August 4th of the same year, a federal judge sentenced the two officers to 30 months in prison; the following year, Rodney King was awarded $3.8 million in his civil trial against six officers.

Since the trials, Rodney King has been arrested for drug infractions, spousal abuse, violence, and driving offenses; he has been in drug rehab and is bankrupt of his civil suit award, as well. Koon and Powell went to Federal Work Camps, and were released in 1995; none of the involved officers work for the L.A.P.D. any more. Williams, the man who beat Reginald Denny, is currently serving a life sentence for the murder of a drug dealer.

As for me, I hope I never see my city burn again.

Defense attorney Michael Stone
demonstrates leg restraints to the jury

JACK KLUGMAN THE ODD COUPLE

Barbara Neuglass v. Jack Klugman (1999)

Barbara Neuglass watches testimony of her former love, Jack Klugman

Ugly, ugly, ugly. That's the only word that comes to mind when I think of the palimony suit Barbara Neuglass brought against her longtime live-in partner, Jack Klugman. Klugman lives up to his *Odd Couple* character, Oscar Madison—he's gruff, curmudgeonly, and pretty much sounds exactly like you would expect him to in court.

After seventeen years together, during which Neuglass said she raised Klugman's children, he dumped her rather unceremoniously. She said that he had promised to take care of her, and sued for half his property, a monthly payment, and other damages—in other words, a divorce settlement for a couple who had never been married. Naturally, Klugman objected.

Neuglass, by her own claim, had been "put out to pasture," and Klugman "treated her like a racehorse," dropping her after she developed bad knees. (Klugman is an avid racehorse fan and even owned a horse who placed third in the 1980 Kentucky Derby. The horse was named "Jaklin Klugman," proving the actor is as humble as he is generous.) He owed her $880,000 because she had made herself available to him for all of the social events he attended over the years; she even belonged to his country club (though her membership ended with their breakup).

As for Klugman, he didn't bother to hide his contempt for her. He sounded curt, nasty, and didn't give a damn about Neuglass; in fact, he said so, claiming he had treated his dog better than he had treated her. Despite the length of the relationship, he said he had never loved her. His proof? He was already married. He and his wife, Brett Somers, separated in 1974 and never bothered to get a divorce. I'm not sure how Neuglass convinced herself that he would marry her after 17 years, but there you go.

THE VERDICT

Not guilty. The judge refused Neuglass's request for palimony. Klugman has been with Peggy Crosby since his breakup with Neuglass in 1992; no reports of what she's doing these days, or whether she's managed to get another country club membership.

MARJORIE KNOLLER
THE BANE OF SAN FRANCISCO

People v. Marjorie Knoller and Robert Noel (2002)

It's a hell of a day when a lawyer is on all fours in the courtroom, barking, and it's actually relevant to a case. In fact, almost every day in the strange case of the San Francisco dog mauling was a hell of a day; from gruesome, to weird, to twisted, to downright creepy, the story just kept getting worse. Or better, depending on which side of the TV camera you're on.

You may remember the grim story: on January 27, 2001, on her way home from grocery shopping, 33-year-old Dianne Whipple was attacked and killed by two Presa Canario mastiffs. The dogs' owners, lawyers Marjorie Knoller and Robert Noel, lived down the hall, and said they had no idea their pets could hurt a flea; apparently, naming the dogs Bane (meaning "a source of harm or ruin") and Hera (Zeus's vengeful wife) was an exercise in irony. Bane was destroyed that night, and Hera two weeks later. The couple was charged with involuntary manslaughter and keeping two mischievous dogs that caused a person's death, and Knoller with the additional cherry of second-degree murder, since she was present at the time of the attack.

At this point, the soap opera begins. The couple showed up on *Good Morning America,* where they appeared unconcerned with Whipple's death, and instead expressed pain for their lost pets. "Ms. Whipple had ample opportunity to move into her apartment," Knoller said. "She could have just slammed the door shut — I would have." Dozens of neighbors came forward with tales of Bane and Hera's viciousness, and their owners' apparent carelessness. Police found evidence connecting them to a dog-fighting ring at Pelican Bay State Prison, where Noel's client, Paul "Cornfed" Schneider, was serving a life sentence. Whipple's partner, Sharon Smith, filed a wrongful death civil suit, becoming the first lesbian domestic partner in the state to do so; Noel said he wasn't concerned about it, because as an unmarried partner, Smith wouldn't have legal standing. During the grand jury hearings, Noel suggested the 110-pound Whipple brought on the attack because the lacrosse coach was either wearing perfume, doing steroids, or on her period. They bore no responsibility, they said.

Nice people we're dealing with here.

And it gets *more* fun: Sexual fantasies—and possibly acts—involving the defendants and their dogs; the revelation that the Jewish couple had adopted Cornfed, a member of the Aryan Brotherhood of Pelican Bay; the Mexican

Robert Noel and Marjorie Knoller at counsel table during jury selection

Mafia, who wanted the dogs for drug labs. . . . At one point, Knoller's eccentric lawyer, Nedra Ruiz, went down on all fours to demonstrate a point. On and on it went; every day, a new twist in the soap opera.

Since the case received daily coverage in San Francisco, the venue was moved to Los Angeles, and that's where I joined the circus. My first impression was that the case was a perfect blend of Northern California meets Southern California. Jim Hammer, a San Francisco D.A., later came out and went on to become a guest legal advisor on the Michael Jackson case, and he's currently a celebrity anchor for CourtTV. The other D.A., former lingerie model Kimberly Guilfoyle, was, at the time, married to Gavin Newsom, soon-to-be pretty boy mayor of San Francisco. She, too, is now a celebrity anchor on CourtTV, and she's also a regular on *Good Morning America* and CNN. One day, a contingent of very young lesbians in leather appeared to show their support for Sharon Smith. Dykes on Bikes, celebrity lawyers . . . it was like Gay Pride Day meets *CSI*.

Seriously, though, I've seen a lot of dreadful photographs in my tenure as a sketch artist, but the Whipple case came close to being the worst. Blood splattered the hallway; Bane went for her neck, presumably severing Whipple's jugular, and it showed. Her sweater was completely shredded and bloodied. Whipple was a small woman, only 110 pounds, and each dog outweighed her.

I'm not really affected by pictures anymore; I've had to develop a pretty strong defense against crime-scene photos. Testimony still gets to me, though. Smith was a sad woman; by the time the trial began, she was seeing someone new, but she still testified as though she had lost the love of her life. She also testified that the dogs had pinned her against the wall once before, and Hera had bitten Whipple's hand. I doubt anyone in the courtroom questioned the veracity of her testimony, especially considering how many more people said the dogs were vicious.

As for the defendants, well, I don't think they had any chance. Noel actually frightened me; he showed no remorse, only arrogance, and acted as though the entire trial was a waste of his time. Though he denied the link to the Aryan Brotherhood, calling him a Nazi doesn't seem too far-fetched. Knoller, on the other hand, looked awful. I suspect she's not all there upstairs; she seemed more

Prosecutor Jim Hammer questions Knoller

110

upset about losing the dogs than the loss of her neighbor's life. (I'm crazy about my two golden retrievers, but I don't think I'd put a human life above theirs.) She claimed to protect Whipple during the fight, but her clothes showed blood that seemed smeared on by her hand. I think she's more or less under Noel's control.

My heart went out to Whipple's parents. Their grief shone through their numb demeanors: At one point, they gave a press conference that their lawyer quickly put an end to. I can't even imagine. . . .

THE VERDICT

Guilty on all counts. The worst of the counts was Knoller's second-degree murder conviction, which a judge reversed in 2002, saying the evidence did not justify the verdict, and granted her a retrial. She and Noel both served four years for involuntary manslaughter and for owning a mischievous animal. Both were released on parole in 2005. In July 2005, the California Supreme Court agreed to review the judge's decision to overturn Knoller's conviction, and her second murder trial began. Smith made legal strides for gays when she was granted permission to file a wrongful death suit on behalf of her domestic partner.

Given the chance to apologize at the sentencing hearing, Knoller and Noel remained silent.

Knoller hides her face as Noel watches forensic specialist describe Whipple's autopsy photos

Ursula and David Karven-Veres at trial for the drowning death of their son

Tommy Lee looks at photo of his pool area

TOMMY LEE
A WALK ON THE WILD SIDE

Ursula Karven v. Tommy Lee (2003)

Two things struck me about the Tommy Lee liability case. One: some millionaires are cheap. Two: some parents trust the drummer of Mötley Crüe to be 100% responsible 100% of the time.

Here's what happened: In 2001, during Tommy Lee's son's birthday pool party, four-year-old Daniel Karven-Veres drowned in the rocker's swimming pool. Shortly thereafter, his parents sued Lee for $10 million on the grounds of premises liability: they believed he was responsible for the death of their child. (His mother, German actress Ursula Karven-Veres, is a star in her home country.)

As a parent and a pool-owner, I was stunned by the general lack of good sense at Lee's party. When my brother, also in the entertainment industry, threw pool parties for his children, he hired *three* lifeguards. After all, why take chances?

Tommy Lee hired caterers, servers, and a doorman to keep out the party crashers, but no lifeguards to watch 25 kids splashing in a pool. His bouncer circulated throughout the party occasionally.

At the poolside, nannies cared for their charges with half an eye or less, and Daniel's nanny literally left him. The 24-year-old Christian Weihs wanted to attend a rock concert and left his charge with another nanny, who proceeded to leave Daniel in the shallow end of the pool as she escorted other kids to the bathroom. Moments later, the little boy drowned in the presence of no less than *ten* adults. Everyone blamed everyone else, which was actually appropriate, all things considered—everyone shared responsibility, in my opinion.

But the case wasn't about everyone. It was about the tattooed, square-jawed drummer of Mötley Crüe, who

may or may not have been legally bound to provide lifeguards. While he was adamant that he was not personally responsible for the child's death, he was also extraordinarily respectful throughout the trial. His appearance brought the only humor to the case. Tattoos creeping up his neck and down his arms, his hair tousled and streaked with yellow, I imagined him asking his lawyer: "What do you wear to court? Does this tie work?"

Gray shirt, black tie, even a handkerchief in the pocket must have been the answer. Lee's probably never looked so playing-it-straight in his life. His bad-boy

reputation still came through (can't hide all the tattoos and the hair, after all), but in general, he showed his intelligence and regret on the stand.

THE VERDICT

Not guilty. Jurors seemed to agree with the idea that the real fault lay with Daniel's parents and nannies, and that Lee couldn't be held solely responsible for his death. In the end, they all understood that when it comes to children, a lifeguard or two is far more important than guarding the velvet rope.

SONDRA LOCKE
HOW TO EAT LUNCH IN THIS TOWN AGAIN

Sondra Locke v. Clint Eastwood (1996)

I t's a classic Hollywood tale: Boy meets girl. Boy and girl fall in love. Boy and girl make movie magic together. Boy breaks up with girl. Girl sues boy for palimony. Boy promises film projects instead of palimony. Boy works behind the scenes to ensure girl never works on another film. Girl sues boy for fraud.

Okay, maybe not *classic*. But anything Clint Eastwood's involved with is bound to become the stuff of Hollywood legend—such as his relationship with Sondra Locke, his 1976 co-star in *The Outlaw Josey Wales*. The two made six movies together during their 15-year relationship, from *Every Which Way But Loose* to *Sudden Impact*. In 1989, the couple finally split, but their relationship wasn't over—not by a long shot.

Later that year, Locke sued Eastwood for palimony for claims up to $1.5 million. Dirty Harry offered a deal that seemed a bargain at the time: instead of the cash, he would see that she would get development deals to direct projects with Warner Brothers. Six years later, she hadn't shot a film, and it seemed as though she never would. That is, until Locke connected the dots: her production deal was a sham. She found out that Eastwood had allegedly secretly agreed to reimburse the studio for any losses incurred by her films.

Locke's attorney, Peggy Garrity, argued the screen legend "dangled a carrot" before her and gave her the development contract in exchange for walking away.

Eastwood's lawyer, Raymond

Sondra Locke taking notes
at the counsel table

Sondra Locke on the stand
in her palimony case

Fisher, countered that Warner had rejected 30 films, which had nothing to do with Eastwood and *everything* to do with salability. The movies just weren't good enough.

Without the movie stars, the case still would've been fascinating (what Eastwood himself called a "dime-novel plot"), but the comparison between Locke's tearful, emotional testimony and Eastwood's brittle monosyllables capti-vated the courtroom. Some actors are very different than the roles they play, but not Eastwood. He remained steely-eyed, tight-lipped, and square-jawed; I kept expecting him to invite Garrity to make his day. His testimony, addressed directly to the jury, possessed the cold solidity of an iceberg. Apparently, Eastwood, when angered in person, is more than stoic; he's glacial.

THE VERDICT

Out-of-court settlement. After one full day of deliberations, the judge sent the jury home. Rumor had it that they would be filing 10-2 for Locke, but that's a moot point—the case was settled out of court with a sealed settlement for Locke. Both parties remain tight-lipped about the case, although their careers tell an inter-esting tale: Clint Eastwood's *Mystic River* was nominated for Best Picture and Best Director in the 2004 Oscars; in 2005, he won both awards for *Million Dollar Baby*. And at the time of this writing, Sondra Locke had made five somewhat unre-markable movies since the case (one for television, and no blockbusters). She directed two of them. Even if she never has lunch in this town again, evidently the "sealed settlement" seems to have made up for it. As Locke herself com-mented, "I don't have to worry about working—let's put it that way."

Clint Eastwood and attorney Raymond Fisher

117

COURTNEY LOVE
ROCKER CHICK EXTRAORDINAIRE

People v. Courtney Love (2004)

Love listens to testimony of a Beverly Hills
police officer involved in her arrest

It used to be that rock 'n' roll stars destroyed hotel rooms. These days, gangsta rappers are the ones hitting the headlines with anger-management issues, and rock stars are more likely to try to stop world hunger than throw an amplifier through a fourth-story window.

Call Courtney Love retro.

At one point during the same year, she was expected in courtrooms in three different cities across the country. From hitting fans with microphones to drugs to unpaid airline tickets, Courtney leaves a path of destruction in her wake that any rocker would admire. But at least she's consistent—every six months or so we can expect a new Courtney antic.

This time around, I was sitting in on a drug charge that stemmed from a breaking and entering/assault charge. Early one morning in April 2004, Love broke into an ex-boyfriend's house in Beverly Hills, and when she found a woman sleeping on his couch, she supposedly chucked a few liquor bottles at her and chased her with a metal flashlight. When the police arrested her, they found illegally-obtained Oxy Contin ("hillbilly heroin," as she called it) in her system and in her purse.

In court, she was the antithesis of a good witness and the epitome of the rocker chick she wants to be: dressed in a flouncy, nearly see-through skirt hiked up to her crotch (underwear optional), her hair styled by rats, braless breasts hanging under low-cut blouses, she looked less like a celebrity than a defendant at a night court. She let us all know the media were devils (although she did talk to someone from *Spin* magazine), and in the brief pauses when she stopped talking, she raised her hand, fourth-grade-style, to be called on by the judge to talk some more.

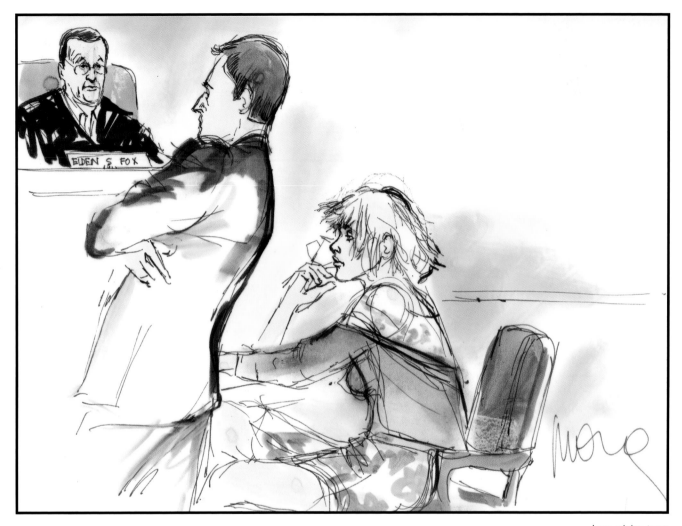

Love wiping tears

Her behavior wasn't much better than that of a cantankerous fourth-grader, actually; she laid across the table a few times, made faces at the police, cried, and talked back to Judge Elden Fox, who also happened to preside over Winona Ryder's shoplifting case. (Winona, of course, was the very height of impeccable fashion in court.)

THE VERDICT

Plea bargain. Love's lawyer—who must love having such a reliably troubled client—convinced her to take a plea bargain in February 2005. She had to go into rehab, perform 100 hours of community service, pay a $1,000 fine, and attend three Narcotics Anonymous meetings a week. As for the assault charge, she pleaded no contest to a lesser charge, and agreed to anger-management counseling, random drug testing, and three years of probation. At one point during a break in the proceedings, Love gave an interview to a reporter in a courthouse toilet in which she said, "The police have a conspiracy against rocker chicks."

In other Love news, she pleaded guilty to disorderly conduct for whacking a fan with a microphone in October 2004, owed her lawyers legal fees as of the same month, and regained custody of her 13-year-old daughter in January 2005. She's since been ordered back to rehab.

Andrew Luster watches physician's testimony

"Jane Doe" testifies at the Luster trial

Andrew Luster
at his trial

CAPTURED!

ANDREW LUSTER
THE LUST FACTOR

People v. Andrew Luster (2003)

Sometimes even the most repellent cases are humorous in their own way. Take Andrew Luster, the Max Factor heir who got his kicks drugging and raping young women. Not a funny guy. Throw in the "Dog," and you have a bizarre made-for-TV movie waiting to happen.

The classic preppie criminal, handsome Andrew Luster made GHB, the date rape drug, famous. He never worked for a living, but he did build a name for himself. As a handsome man in his mid-30s, Luster brought at least three women into his home, drugged them into unconsciousness, and, unbeknownst to them, filmed himself having sex with them. In fairly short order, the women approached the police, the police arrested him, and the trust-funder faced charges for rape.

The predictability of some people truly astounds me. The formula for the young, privileged man in court is foolproof: day one, he's cocky, arrogant, and all but rolling his eyes at the riffraff that surrounds him. Fast forward a few months, and the same man needs a shave, a haircut, slouches in his chair, and is more or less begging the aforementioned riffraff for mercy. It happened with the Menendez brothers, with Patrick McNaughton, and Andrew Luster was no exception.

The difference was, Luster took a vacation in the meantime.

Even his defense was appallingly arrogant—the girls *wanted* it, he said. They did the drugs with him and liked it. They weren't really unconscious during the sex; they were acting out a rape fantasy. He wanted to be a film director, and they were trying to take advantage of his wealth. Poor rich boy.

The trial recessed during the 2002 Christmas holidays. Luster was out on $1 million bond, on home detention, and we had no reason not to expect him back in court on January 6th. But sometime on that Saturday, January 4th, he disappeared from his Mussel Shoals beach house. Poof—just like that. The police sent out an All Points Bulletin, to no avail, and the next day, famed bounty hunter Duane "Dog" Chapman said he would land the man back in court. "This one has become personal," Chapman declared. "If one of the victims comes up to me and says, 'Dog, thank you,' that's it. I'm paid."

In the meantime, the trial continued *in absentia,* and the rest of us sat and listened to painful testimony from the women Luster raped. They made a bad choice in going home with someone they just met, no doubt there; but to find out later that you had been raped—and not only that, but *filmed*? And then to hear the defense say they enjoyed it, that they were only pretending, must have been incredibly painful.

THE VERDICT

Guilty. Only three weeks after Luster's disappearance, the jury convicted him of raping three women and drugging them with GHB, and a short while later, he was sentenced to 124 years in prison.

Meanwhile, an American couple had apparently been in contact with Luster. They met him while vacationing in Puerto Vallarta, Mexico, and while sharing photos with a friend, they identified him as the fugitive. They contacted the Dog, and then the FBI, who all headed to Puerto Vallarta. In a bizarre twist, when the Dog and his team of bounty hunters captured Luster, they were all arrested as well—along with the television crew they had brought along to film their heroics. It seems that bounty hunting is illegal in Mexico, so as far as the Mexican authorities were concerned, what the Dog was actually doing was kidnapping Luster.

The Dog ended up in jail, but so did Luster; he was then brought back to the United States to begin serving out his 124-year term. The Dog, meanwhile, was eventually released and returned to the U.S. within a month of Luster's return, where he has since hosted a show on A&E called—what else?—*Dog the Bounty Hunter.*

Imelda Marcos

IMELDA MARCOS
QUEEN OF QUALITY FOOTWEAR

United States of America v. Imelda Marcos (1989)

Quick, what's the first word that comes to your mind when you think of Imelda Marcos? Is it shoes? I knew it.

In her home country of the Philippines, Imelda wasn't just known as a collector of designer footwear—she was called the "Steel Butterfly," the beautiful wife and confidant of dictator Ferdinand Marcos. During her husband's 30-year regime, Imelda instituted social welfare and assistance programs, but apparently goodwill can't always balance the effects of being half of the most corrupt regime in the Pacific. When she and her husband fled to Hawaii in 1986, opposition forces found thousands of shoes in her closets (size 8 1/2), proving to her impoverished nation and to the world that to Imelda, fashion was more important than philanthropy.

I witnessed the original federal lawsuit in 1989, when Imelda stood trial for concealing ownership of U.S. property and other goods, purchased with stolen Philippine government funds. She lived up to her Steel Butterfly moniker. She wore a lovely black wool dress and a *huge* gold rosary on her neck, displaying a cross as big as her shoe collection. A Filipino flag pin adorned her breast, and her lacquered pompadour framed a face of such imperious austerity that I expected someone to scrape at her toes any moment. She definitely didn't look like the type who would go crazy at a Neiman Marcus last-call sale.

The themes of church and state were intertwined throughout the trial; she talked about God a great deal, and I suspected she was hoping for divine intervention. I always find it amusing when defendants show up in court wearing crosses—Farrah Fawcett wore the biggest

cross I'd ever seen, Winona wore a cross, as did Anna Nicole; Courtney Love also wore a cross, although I suspect that was an ironic fashion statement. Imelda's cross was clearly a plea for divine intervention, and evidently, it worked.

THE VERDICT

Not guilty. The defense's claim that her husband was solely responsible for the crimes worked, and since Ferdinand had already died, no one paid the piper for the corruption. Imelda returned to the Philippines in 1991; after an unsuccessful presidential bid, she was sentenced to 18 to 24 years in prison for corruption. Her October 1998 appeal succeeded, ensuring Imelda's freedom. As Imelda herself said, "They went into my closets looking for skeletons, but thank God, all they found were shoes, beautiful shoes."

And it all comes back to the shoes.

Every damn day, the first thing we all did was check out her feet. Would they be Ferragamo? Chanel? Givenchy? Alas, all of my drawings end at her lap, so I have no permanent record of her choices for court; all I can say is that they were black. Fortunately, in 2001, she opened the Marikina City Footwear Museum in Manila. It's the shoe capital of the Philippines, and while the museum includes shoes from other famous leaders, the bulk of the collection is Imelda's. Next time you're in the neighborhood, be sure to check them out.

LEE MARVIN
PILLOW TALK, OR PALIMONY?

Michelle Triola v. Lee Marvin (1979)

Back when Reagan was on the verge of becoming our next president, I took a chance on a new career, and NBC took a chance on me. I'd never been a courtroom sketch artist; I'd never even served for jury duty. Except for the actual drawing part, I had no idea what I was doing when I walked into California's first palimony suit.

Lee Marvin, star of such manly films as *The Dirty Dozen* and *The Man Who Shot Liberty Valance,* dated girlfriend Michelle Triola for several years. (He was still married to his wife, Pamela Feeley, throughout his relationship with Triola.) When Marvin and Triola broke up in 1977, she filed suit against him, claiming that he said he would support her for the rest of her life. In legalspeak, she alleged that while "the parties lived together they would combine their efforts and earnings and would share equally any and all property accumulated as a result of their efforts whether individual or combined." In other words, just because they weren't married didn't mean she didn't deserve something.

I entered the case nervous as hell. Fortunately, another courtroom artist, Bill Robles, was kind enough to guide me along—he helped me choose where to sit, gave advice, and answered my questions. In other words, he helped me bluff my way through my first day in court.

THE VERDICT

Not guilty. The court held in favor of the defendant, Lee Marvin. Later, though, the California Supreme Court reversed the decision, holding that if the plaintiff can establish an *implied* partnership or contract, they might be due some compensation.

The new law opened the door for many such "palimony" cases in the future—some of which are right here in this book. And it also opened the door for my career as a courtroom artist.

Todd McCormick in shackles

McCormick's lawyer addresses the judge

UNITED STATES MAGISTRATE JUDGE
HON. JAMES W. McMAHON

CAPTURED!

TODD McCORMICK
STONED IN BEL-AIR

People v. Todd McCormick (1999)

McCormick breaks down and
is comforted by his attorney

Who says you need a few acres of land to cultivate a full crop of marijuana plants? Some people just need a mansion in Bel-Air. Imagine: you rent a tidy little mansion, nestled in the hills among the stars and swimming pools, take out all the furniture, and install heat-lamps in every room, thus converting the entire house into a giant greenhouse.

Then you truck in 4,000 marijuana plants, all of which are for your own personal medicinal use. Then you get arrested.

I imagine most folks outside of Los Angeles—certainly outside of California—have never heard of Todd McCormick, but he's something of a local legend. His life hasn't been easy. He had cancer nine times before he was 10 and he still suffers from cancer. He grew up to be one of California's most vocal advocates for the use of medical marijuana. (In his case, he uses it to reduce cancer-related pain and increase his appetite.) After his arrest, he was not permitted to use any form of marijuana, not even Marinol, a synthetic prescription form of THC, marijuana's active ingredient.

Why was I there? Because Woody Harrelson had shown personal interest in his case. The former *Cheers* star had made no secret of his love for all things marijuana, and not only did he post the $500,000 bail for McCormick, he also testified on his behalf, showing up to the courtroom dressed in a shirt made of hemp. Other witnesses were equally as colorful, quite literally—one testified with bright green spiked hair and an orange beard.

After undergoing months of drug tests to ensure that McCormick had not been using Marinol, pot, or any other THC-related products (he would be in violation of his bail if he had), the judge in McCormick's case ruled that any mention of medical necessity would not be permitted in court, a serious blow to the defense's case. Including necessity meant he was treating serious side effects of cancer; leaving it out meant he was a guy with 4,000 marijuana plants in a Bel-Air mansion. The ruling was in direct opposition to a Ninth Circuit Court of Appeals decision only two months earlier—they unanimously ruled that medical necessity is a viable defense. Todd and his co-defendant, Peter McWilliams—a critically ill AIDS patient who has since passed away—faced 10 years in jail. (McWilliams said his role in the pot-growing was to pay a book advance to McCormick, who planned to write books on medical marijuana.)

THE VERDICT

Guilty. In November, 1999, McCormick and McWilliams pleaded guilty to conspiracy to manufacture and distribute marijuana; all other charges were dropped. While serving his five-year sentence, McCormick was repeatedly put into solitary confinement for using marijuana in prison. After serving four years, he was released to a halfway house in December, 2003.

In June of 2005, the Supreme Court declared that the federal government can prosecute medical marijuana users, even when state laws permit doctor-prescribed use of the drug, effectively halting medical marijuana's chances of legality. I suspect more than a few people are currently breaking federal law.

STANLEY K WEISBERG
JUDGE

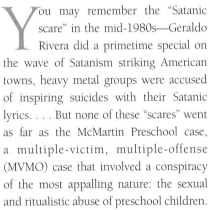
Child on witness stand as Ray Buckey looks on

Ray Buckey and his mother, Peggy Buckey, listen to testimony in preschool molestation case

McMartin Preschool
A 20th-Century
Witch-Hunt

People v. Ray Buckey et al. (1990)

You may remember the "Satanic scare" in the mid-1980s—Geraldo Rivera did a primetime special on the wave of Satanism striking American towns, heavy metal groups were accused of inspiring suicides with their Satanic lyrics. . . . But none of these "scares" went as far as the McMartin Preschool case, a multiple-victim, multiple-offense (MVMO) case that involved a conspiracy of the most appalling nature: the sexual and ritualistic abuse of preschool children.

The twist? No evidence. The accusations started in 1983, with Judy Johnson, the mother of young Matthew Johnson, whom she believed had been abused by workers at the family-owned and run McMartin Preschool. On the basis of little evidence—Matthew's red and itchy anus—she demanded an investigation, sparking what became *the* witch

hunt of the 20th century. Many parents in Manhattan Beach began to suspect that their children had also been abused, and they all set out to prove their suspicions true.

The case involved nearly 400 children who had allegedly been abused at McMartin. I say "allegedly" because none of the allegations—ranging from the threat of being eaten by lions to oral sex to chopping off the heads of babies—were supported by physical evidence. Every shred of evidence came from a series of interviews conducted by social workers, not qualified pediatricians or psychiatrists, who were later shown to be "leading" the young children to the "correct" answers. The children were suspected of covering up when they said nothing happened (and, indeed, most children said just that at first), and were positively rein-

forced when they agreed that they had been abused. In other words, the adults had been so convinced of their children's victimization that the children believed they had been victimized themselves.

In 1984, Ray Buckey, his sister Peggy Ann, his mother, Peggy, grandmother, Virginia McMartin, and three other teachers were arrested for sexually abusing the children in their care.

As the investigation and case wore on, Judy Johnson was diagnosed with alcoholism and paranoid schizophrenia; when her husband left her, she accused him of sodomizing Matthew, as well. Matthew eventually went to live with relatives. She died in 1985 of conditions related to alcoholism. Despite her obvious incredibility as the initial accuser—and the release of Virginia, Peggy Ann, and the additional three teachers due to

lack of evidence—the war against McMartin raged on for five more years.

THE VERDICT

Not guilty. After seven long years and $16 million—the most expensive trial in American history to date—the jury both deadlocked on some charges and acquitted on others; Peggy was acquitted on all counts after spending two years in jail (the jury said afterwards that the interviews had so tainted the children's memories that they couldn't determine what had really happened). In 1990, after having spent five years in jail, Ray's second trial resulted in a deadlock on all counts, and the prosecutors dropped the charges. The McMartin Preschool was subsequently leveled later that year.

Attorney Howard Weitzman, representing Allergan, finds himself face to face with (former) friend Irena Medavoy

Arnold Klein, MD, holds his walking stick with silver head, while waiting to testify

IRENA MEDAVOY
EXTREME MAKEOVER, L.A. EDITION

Irena Medavoy v. Dr. Arnold Klein (2004)

High-powered attorneys, former studio heads, cosmetic surgery, migraine headaches, and Vanna White: you would be hard-pressed to find a lawsuit more L.A. than the case of Irena Medavoy's Botox mishap.

The socialite (her husband, Mike Medavoy, is the former head of Tri-Star Pictures) suffered terrible migraine headaches, so naturally, she went to Dr. Arnold Klein, dermatologist and cosmetic surgeon to the stars. He administered Botox—the botulinum toxin that freeze-frames smiles for life—an unconventional treatment, to be sure, but one that had apparently cured other women's migraines. Not only did it *not* work, but she suffered even more headaches, nausea, and muscle pain.

The Medavoys filed suit against Dr. Klein and Allergan, Inc., the pharmaceutical firm that produced the Botox,

alleging that he hadn't informed Irena of the risks, that Allergan retained him as a consultant, and that poor Mike had suffered emotional damage from losing the companionship of his wife.

The courtroom was as L.A.-incestuous as it gets. Powerhouse attorney Howard Weitzman defended Allergan, ironic in itself because he and Mike used to yacht together. Vanna White, a close friend of Irena's, showed up to testify on her behalf, and she looked simply naked without all her buy-a-vowel makeup. In fact, I was in the hall when she was called to the stand, so I didn't hear her name, and it took about five minutes after sketching her for me to realize who she was! Dr. Klein carried a walking stick with a big cat for a handle, a gift from none other than Michael Jackson. (I feel I can safely assume the gift was in thanks for years of faithful service.)

Picture it: the jury, mostly minority, working-class people listening patiently as Irena Medavoy, the wife of a studio head in $500-shoes and a $1,000 purse, related her tale of woe.

She went to 113 doctors for her migraines and assorted ailments that plague her constantly—113! Her cosmetic surgery-cum-headache cure made her hurt! She couldn't perform her wifely duties! For the love of all that's good and

kind in the world, *she couldn't even go to the Golden Globes party!* Terrible, really. I'm surprised no one was brought to tears.

THE VERDICT

Not guilty. Allergan's product was not flawed, and Dr. Klein simply gave her what she wanted: a big ol' shot of botulism. She and her husband are, of course, appealing. Maybe next time she'll use liposuction to cure her sinus problems!

Irena Medavoy listens to her attorney, Jeffrey Benice

A view of the counsel table at the beginning of the Menendez Brothers' trial

Erik and Lyle in button-down shirts watch their attorney, Leslie Abramson, address the court

MENENDEZ BROTHERS
ALL IN THE FAMILY

People v. Lyle and Erik Menendez (1995)

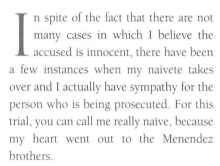

In spite of the fact that there are not many cases in which I believe the accused is innocent, there have been a few instances when my naivete takes over and I actually have sympathy for the person who is being prosecuted. For this trial, you can call me really naïve, because my heart went out to the Menendez brothers.

What a *weird* case. I'd come home one day, feeling the enormity of their tragic lives, and tell my husband that I didn't blame them; the next day, I'd tell my husband they deserved to burn for the atrocity they had committed. He must've thought I was as crazy as they were. The entire case boiled down to one question: Were the boys driven to murder? Or were they cold-blooded killers?

On August 20, 1989, Kitty and José Menendez were dozing in the family room of their $4-million, 23-room Beverly Hills mansion when they were both shot at point-blank range. When the killers ran out of ammunition, and Kitty still lived, they returned to their car, reloaded their twelve-gauge shotguns, finished the job, collected the shell casings, and left the house. Two hours later, the local 911 dispatcher received a phone call from 21-year-old Lyle Menendez, reporting the murder of his parents.

Within four days, Lyle and 18-year-old Erik drowned their sorrows at the mall in a spree sponsored by their father's $650,000 insurance policy: they bought new cars, designer clothes, jewelry, and dropped $15,000 alone on Rolex watches and money clips. Fearing "mobsters," they stayed in hotel after hotel at the expense of LIVE Entertainment, where their father had been the president. In five days, the boys ran up an $8,800 bill at the Bel-Air Hotel, and also had LIVE pay for limousines and bodyguards. By October, they had both rented new apartments, spent $24,000 on stereo equipment, purchased a Porsche and a Jeep Wrangler, and ran up a $90,000 tab on their father's American Express card. Lyle bought a restaurant in Princeton for $550,000; Erik lost $40,000 to back a concert at the L.A. Palladium, and hired a private tennis coach for $60,000 a year. All in all, odd activity by children wracked with grief.

The police weren't having such a swell time. José had made a lot of enemies during his career; he was a controlling, occasionally unethical businessman, so the list of murder suspects kept growing. When detective Les Zoeller interviewed family friend Peter Wiere, he added two more—the picture-perfect sons who had called the police that night. Zoeller examined their freewheeling spending behavior and paid Erik a visit. Afterwards, an anxious Erik met with his psychotherapist, Jerome Oziel, and said, "We did it. We killed our parents."

Lyle joined Erik at Oziel's office a short while later, infuriated with his brother; Erik confessed to everything, from drawing their inspiration from *The Billionaire Boys Club* television movie, to how they believed they would be disinherited from their father's will, to the careful planning of the perfect murder.

After a lengthy investigation, Lyle was arrested on March 7, 1990; when Erik returned home from a tennis trip to Israel on March 11th, police greeted him at the airport. Their family immediately

retained the fiercest trial lawyer in Los Angeles: Leslie Abramson, who would represent Erik. Jill Lansing, who had been a public defender until recently, represented Lyle.

They waited for their trial for three years, biding their time in jail, segregated from other prisoners. Erik became suicidal and began telling tragic tales of his youth to a psychiatrist, stories which became the bedrock of their defense.

The first trial began in the summer of 1993. Three months earlier, the judge had decided to combine the trials, meaning two juries would hear all of the arguments and evidence. Abramson said the boys would admit to murder, but that they were driven to it by their parents' abuse. After consulting with the author of a book about children who kill their parents, Abramson tried to paint the perfect picture of two polite, misunderstood boys. By this time, they were 22- and 25-year-old men, but she engineered their clothes and behavior in court to reinforce the picture of innocent children. Calling them her "boys," she dressed them in Ralph Lauren sweaters and pinstriped polo shirts in ice-cream colors. They looked like students at a prep school in a 1980s teen movie.

They showed up just a bit late to court every day; in jail, you're not permitted to have anything as luxurious as a toupee, and the prematurely bald Lyle had to fasten on his hair upon arrival at the courthouse. Throughout the trial, Abramson touched them both constantly, patting them, petting their necks and backs, acting like a concerned relative instead of a tiger of a trial lawyer. And it all played out before television cameras—the judge permitted Court TV to film the first trial.

In the mid-'90s, America was just beginning its obsession with Court TV. Between O.J. Simpson and Rodney King,

everyone loved the idea of these preppie young men murdering their parents in cold blood. By the end of the trial, I didn't know what to believe. Accounts of extreme sexual abuse made me pity Erik; on the other hand, Lyle's acting on the 911 call seemed terribly cold and calculated. Apparently the juries felt the same way. Both juries deadlocked in January, 1994, and the judge declared mistrials.

In October, 1995, the second trial began; this time the brothers would be tried together. At this point, six years had passed since their parents' murder, the Menendez estate was destitute, and Leslie Abramson was defending Erik on the pub-

lic's tax dollars. This time around, the judge did not allow television cameras, declared that only one jury would decide the fates of the brothers, and limited the number of witnesses who would testify to abuse. The judge was even tough on the courtroom artists—he allowed one seat for an artist, which was the last seat in the row on the right side. Closing my eyes is the only thing that would worsen that view.

THE VERDICT

Guilty. The absence of the media spectacle, a new prosecutor, and a new trial did the trick—on March 20th, after only four days of deliberation, the jury found Lyle

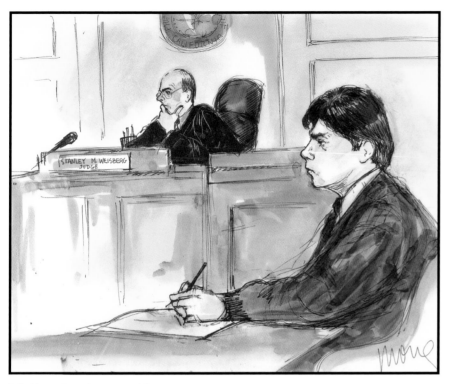

Lyle Menendez takes notes while
Judge Weisberg listens to testimony

Erik testifies about early childhood traumas

Judge Stanley Weisberg

and Erik guilty on all counts. Luckily for the boys, though, they spared their lives: life in prison would be their sentence, not the death penalty. In 1996, Lyle married Ann Eriksson; they divorced after a year. In 1999, Erik married Tammi Ruth Saccoman in a telephone ceremony at the California State Prison. In 2003, Lyle married Rebecca Sneed in a ceremony at the California State Prison. Leslie Abramson is now an occasional commentator on Court TV and *Nightline*.

After everything, one image remains burned into my mind—not the boys in their polo shirts, not the bloody shirts or the cameras from Court TV. What haunts me is the bowl of melted ice cream, sitting on the coffee table next to Kitty's bullet-ridden body. A checkbook and bill for Erik's parking at UCLA lay next to the bowl. At some point that evening, I thought, she had been eating ice cream and paying for Erik's parking, having no idea what was in store for her and her family.

PEOPLE V. LYLE AND ERIK MENENDEZ

HON. EDWARD RAFE

CAPTURED!

Patrick Naughton looking a
bit disheveled in his jail overalls

Patrick Naughton with his attorneys,
Anthony Brooklier and Donald Marks

PATRICK NAUGHTON
FANTASY AND FELONY

United States of America v. Patrick Naughton (1999)

In the case of Heidi Fleiss, lust was an adult activity engaged in behind closed doors. In the case of Patrick Naughton, though, lust was much darker, the most insidious of sins—one involving a deviant adult and the potential loss of a child's innocence.

Naughton personified the American Dream at the height of the Internet bubble: the 35-year-old wunderkind was the senior executive of Disney's Infoseek search engine. During his short tenure at Infoseek, he apparently spent his spare time as "hotseattle," chatting with young girls and trading nude photos in the "dad&daughterssex" Internet Relay Chat room. One girl, "KrisLA," chatted with him for six months before agreeing to meet him on the beach near the Santa Monica pier on September 16, 1999.

Imagine the married man's surprise when he discovered that the braid-ed, cap-and-overall-clad KrisLA was an undercover police officer. Arrested on the spot as a "traveler"—a criminal who finds children on the Web and then tries to meet them for sex—Naughton's suburban existence was crushed beneath his secret Internet life.

Naughton's transformation was similar to that of Heidi Fleiss. He began his four-day testimony in designer suits, perfectly coiffed hair, and a confident attitude, and was visibly brought down a few notches when he had to show up in a government-issued jumpsuit and three-day beard growth after being in jail for a long three-day weekend. His body language transformed from an arrogant young executive to that of a humiliated pedophile caught in the act.

Patrick Naughton, confident and
well-dressed, testifying at his trial

Attorney Donald Marks questions investigators, while Naughton looks on

Federal Judge Edward Rafeedie addresses Patrick Naughton

Prosecutor Patricia Donahue shows photo of Santa Monica Pier, where Naughton met the "girl"

Naughton's confidence appears to be slipping once the case gets under way

THE VERDICT

Guilty . . . and guilty by plea bargain. On December 16, 1999, Naughton was convicted of possessing child pornography, but his "fantasy defense" apparently did the trick. (The fantasy defense stated that because nothing on the Internet is reality, because it's all "virtual reality," that it's actually *all* fantasy.) After three days of deliberation, the jurors deadlocked on the charge that he crossed state lines to engage in sex with a minor and used the Internet to set up the meeting.

The mistrial led to a second trial, which ended with Naughton's guilty plea: he *had* crossed state lines to have sex with a minor. In August, 2000, he was sentenced to nine months of house arrest, a $20,000 fine, and five years of probation. His far greater sentence was the loss of his job, his family, and of the American Dream that had driven him to the top of Disney's e-business.

Today, he's apparently trying to make restitution in the best way he knows how: he now works with law enforcement to track down Internet pedophiles.

DOLLY PARTON
AMERICA'S SWEETHEART

Neil Goldberg v. Dolly Parton (1985)

A spoonful of sugar helps the medicine go down—and sometimes, it wins the case. Dolly Parton is exactly what she appears to be: cute as a button and sweet as sugar. With her cotton-candy hair, stiletto heels, tiny stature, and Southern lilt, I can't imagine any jury would convict her, even if she had been caught with a gun in her hand and blood on her rhinestones.

In a nutshell, the case was about copyright infringement: two songwriters, Mr. and Mrs. Neil Goldberg, claimed Parton stole the song "9 to 5." Their song, called "Money World," had a chorus that went "got the people working nine to five/got them hustlin' just to stay alive/got them working nights and overtime/got them living only to survive." Compare that to "working nine to five, what a way to make a livin'/barely gettin' by, it's all takin' and no givin'…" The case itself was

fairly unremarkable—compared to dogs eating people and serial killing, anyway—so I'm not even sure why they bothered with a trial. A low-key hippie type accuses America's sweetheart of stealing? Not bloody likely. At one point, Parton played the song on her guitar; at another, Goldberg played the eight notes he said were his. A deaf fool could've heard the similarity, but Parton's lawyers said the progression was so ordinary that they couldn't prove he was the original writer. Whether either songwriter was insulted by the apparent lack of originality, I don't know. Parton's business partners, Jane Fonda and Tom Hayden, also testified on her behalf.

My favorite moment came not in the courtroom, but in the bathroom. I was washing my hands during a break when the lady herself approached me. "I like your drawings," she said in her soft

Parton watches proceedings
from the counsel table

Southern voice. "May I have one? I'll buy it." She whipped out her checkbook, wrote me a check, and then she went to use the lavatory (I promised to mail the illustration to her). It's the first and last business transaction I've ever conducted in a ladies' room.

THE VERDICT

Not guilty. I'm still undecided about whether I think Ms. Parton stole the song, as the notes could have been written by anyone, but I'd hate to be the one to tarnish her rhinestone tiara. Especially since she's so gosh-darn nice.

Ramirez in handcuffs entering the courtroom

Richard Ramirez at counsel table

RICHARD RAMIREZ
THE LONG, HOT SUMMER

People v. Richard Ramirez (1989)

People often ask me what it's like being in a room with criminals, and most of the time, it's just another day at work—with all the media hoopla, it even feels vaguely unreal. But that wasn't the case with the Night Stalker.

In June of 1984, Richard Ramirez slipped in through the window of 79-year-old Jennie Vincow's home and repeatedly stabbed and slashed her. The murder signaled the start of a reign of terror that would keep Southern California sweating buckets—literally and figuratively—for the next 15 months. In March, he murdered four people; in May, he murdered two people, and raped a woman while her son watched; in June, five more attacks, three resulting in death; in July, four dead and two who lived to tell the tale; in August, one more dead, all in the Los Angeles area. At one point in late August, he escaped to Lake Merced, near the Bay Area, and shot two people,

killing one and paralyzing the other; a week later, he attacked two more people in Mission Viejo, halfway between Los Angeles and San Diego.

I remember it as the hottest summer of the 1980s, but that may be because of the gripping terror. We slept with our windows closed, locked our doors, suffered in the sweltering heat for fear of the "Night Stalker" paying our families a visit. Every neighborhood bore wanted posters; we all knew his face from sketches, but still, he continued to rape, rob, murder, and assault Californians.

For my husband's birthday on the weekend of August 31, 1985, we took our children and went to a cabin in Lake Arrowhead; we had hoped it would release us from the fear, but I still couldn't sleep without every window and door locked tight. We broiled in the heat, but not for long—that was the very weekend that Ramirez stepped off a bus in East Los

Angeles and saw his own name and picture plastered on every newspaper in the bus station. Police descended on the area, and as Ramirez tried to disappear into the Hispanic community, he met only hate and resistance: the citizens of East L.A. hit him with barbeque tongs, put him in headlocks, fought him out of their cars, and, eventually, an angry mob released a year's worth of terror on the killer. They pinned him to the ground, police arrested him, and his reign ended—14 murders in all.

But my experience with Ramirez didn't end there. I was in the early stages of my courtroom-sketching career, and the Night Stalker's preliminary hearing was one of my first cases for ABC television. It was the most eerie, unsettling experience of my life. I sat directly behind the defense, and occasionally, Ramirez turned to look at me and watch me draw. He smiled with the crooked teeth that had been one of his identifying marks (this was before the state paid for him to get his teeth fixed). My blood ran cold. I couldn't avoid looking at him; I had to draw him! I began taking glances, then looking elsewhere, hoping he wouldn't see me drawing his image. If he saw I was sketching, he watched me, so I began covering my face. I didn't want to attract his attention,

and I certainly didn't want him burning my face onto his memory. There are few people I'd classify as evil, but malevolence came off of him in waves.

THE VERDICT

Guilty. After several delays (one juror was murdered in an unrelated crime, and another had to be replaced for falling asleep), Ramirez was found guilty of 14 murders and 31 other felonies related to his crime spree; 19 of those counts were with "special circumstances," making him more than eligible for the death penalty. On November 9, 1989, he was sentenced to death no fewer than 19 times. His reaction? "You do not understand me. I do not expect you to. You are not capable of it. I am beyond your experience. I am beyond good and evil. Legions of the night, night breed, repeat not the errors of night prowler and show no mercy. I will be avenged. Lucifer dwells within us all. . . . No big deal. Death always comes with the territory. I'll see you in Disneyland."

Seven years later, on October 3, 1996, Richard Ramirez married freelance magazine editor Doreen Lioy in a prison ceremony. Her band was gold; his was platinum. The reason for their different rings: Ramirez says Satanists don't wear gold.

Near

AHMED RESSAM
NEW YEAR'S EVE BLAST

United States Government v. Ahmed Ressam (2005)

Sometimes, a case gets blown so far out of proportion that the media circus gets as much coverage as the case itself. And sometimes, cases get so little coverage in proportion to the crime that it's a wonder they're covered at all.

On December 14, 1999, Ahmed Ressam, an Algerian man in his mid-30s, tried to cross the Canadian-U.S. border at Port Angeles, Washington. A pretty, sweet-looking border patrolwoman followed her regular routine: checked his passport, examined the car, and asked him to pop the trunk. She found enough bombs (made in olive oil bottles, I believe) to blow up a small building. Ressam was arrested.

At first, authorities believed he had planned to blow up the Seattle Space Needle, but it turns out Ressam had planned to drive all the way to Los Angeles and blow up LAX during the mil-lennial celebrations. Instead, he landed in jail and, in hopes of a short sentence, began cooperating with authorities.

At the time, Ressam's arrest made a small splash; he was more or less a dumb, wannabe terrorist jumping on the millennial bandwagon. I thought the case was incredibly serious—he had planned to blow up my airport!—but some other journalists seemed exasperated, as though covering this case was a waste of time. Ressam, himself, was a puny, frightened-looking guy, but the biggest entities in the United States—the F.B.I., the C.I.A.—were fighting over him. He wasn't able to get a fair hearing anywhere in Washington, so they moved the entire trial—judge included—to the federal court in L.A. He only spoke French and Arabic, and translators followed him every step of the way; French-Canadian television covered the trial in detail.

A wide shot of the federal
courtroom handling the
multinational trial

The Border Patrol agent, Diana Dean, who stopped Ressam while crossing into Washington, testifies in court

THE VERDICT

Guilty. Despite the perception that he was an unimportant nut, we had all come to realize how important his capture, and subsequent cooperation, was. His disclosures described Al-Qaeda sleeper cells in the United States (information included in the president's daily briefing on August 6, 2001, titled "Bin Laden Determined to Strike in U.S."); he helped put away Mokhtar Haouari, who helped plan the logistics of the LAX plan, and he also provided information on more than 100 suspected terrorists, which in turn helped authorities shut down clandestine Al-Qaeda cells, and exposed organizational secrets.

Unfortunately, when Ressam realized his sentence would be longer than he expected, he stopped cooperating. He also said he was mistreated and bullied in custody, and didn't believe he would ever received fair treatment from the United States. The 38-year-old was sentenced to 22 years in prison—halfway between what the prosecution and defense wanted.

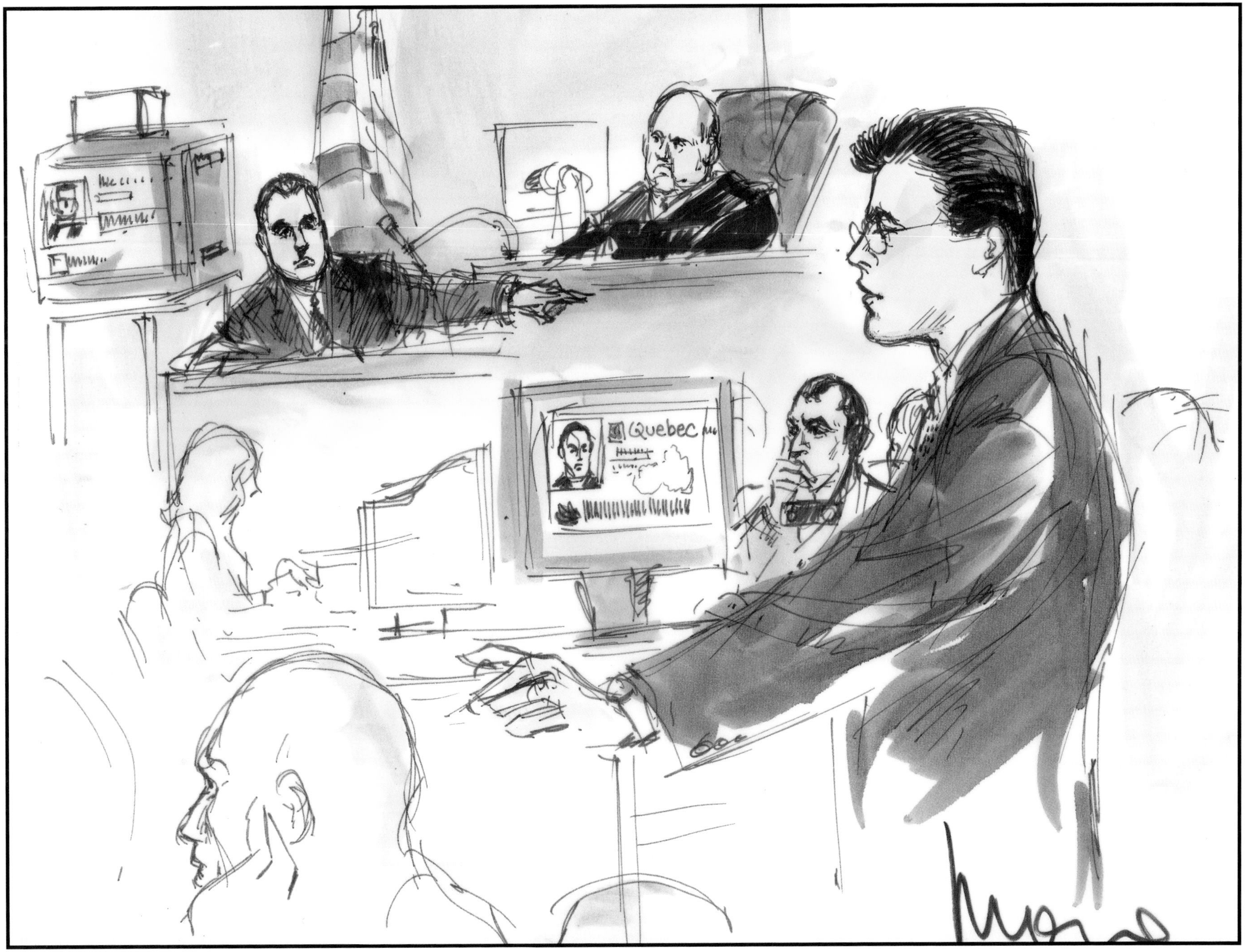
Quebec

WINONA RYDER
REALITY BITES

People v. Winona Ryder (2002)

Winona, Winona, Winona. Hollywood's "It Girl" of the late '80s and '90s—the petite, porcelain-skinned star of *Heathers, Reality Bites, Edward Scissorhands,* and other popular films—may go down in history as the wealthiest shoplifter ever to get nabbed in Saks. On December 12, 2001, the actress tried to leave Saks Fifth Avenue Beverly Hills with more than $5000 worth of stolen goods. Designer, of course.

While cameras weren't allowed in the courtroom, evening news did treat us to a different shot of Ryder's famous face—a black-and-white, security-camera view of her small frame wandering past the counter of Saks, bags in hand. Even more embarrassing for Ryder were the garments themselves: designer clothes and purses, shot through with holes where sensor tags had been cut out. The final insult: A pair of orange plastic scissors found in Ryder's handbag.

As a former fashion illustrator, the case was a dream for me, as it involved high fashion; I eagerly covered Ryder's couture looks, a new one every day. On her first day in court, the pixie-like woman dressed in a hot pink sweater and floral skirt—more suited for a picnic than a grand theft trial. I mentioned this to one of her attorneys, and the next day, she wore a low-key black suit with a white collar. (She likes to mix her designers—wear a new Prada with an old Chanel.)

An especially bizarre aspect of the case was my backseat expert "testimony"—every day, reporters would seek my fashion expertise on the cut and style of her skirt, the name of the designer, why she wore her sweater in a particular way.

Winona Ryder wearing a sling into court after being jostled by cameras and officers while being accompanied into the building

Prosecutor Ann Rundle displays to the jury scissors found in Ryder's purse

Winona Ryder watches testimony by Saks security guard

They were fascinated by everything but the trial itself, which, to me, was a pretty open-and-shut shoplifting case. As prosecutor Ann Rundle proclaimed, "She came. She stole. She left."

THE VERDICT

Guilty: Grand theft and vandalism. Not guilty: Commercial burglary. Ryder was sentenced to 480 hours of community service, a $10,000 fine, and counseling, presumably for kleptomania. "If you steal again, you will go to jail," were Judge Elden Fox's final words.

The real sentence, though, was the boost to Ryder's career. Cutting holes in blouses and sweaters didn't just get her face splashed across the evening news—it also got her into fashion magazines all over the world. She appeared on the cover of *W Magazine* in a "Free Winona" t-shirt, hosted *Saturday Night Live*, and was hired by Marc Jacobs to be his next spokesperson. The designer himself has made sure she'll never have to steal another sweater again.

Attorney Mark Geragos holds Saks shopping bag while discussing Ryder's appearance on security footage. Photos of dressing room shutters are in the foreground.

Arnold Schwarzenegger testifies at the
trial of photographers Giles Harrison
and Andrew O'Brien

Arnold Schwarzenegger gestures at how
close the paparazzi came to hitting his car

Maria Shriver on the witness stand

MARIA SHRIVER & ARNOLD SCHWARZENEGGER
A TRAPPED TERMINATOR

People v. Giles Harrison and Andrew O'Brien (1998)

Many years ago, saying "harassment" and "Schwarzenegger" in the same context meant paparazzi, not politics. In the spring of 1997, while Arnold Schwarzenegger and a pregnant Maria Shriver tried to drop off their son at school, British photographers boxed in the family's car and snapped away. (Schwarzenegger had recently had heart surgery, and the photographers wanted the first post-surgery photographs.) Giles Harrison was charged with reckless driving and two counts of false imprisonment; Andrew O'Brien was charged with four counts of false imprisonment and battery because he shoved people who were attempting to help the Hollywood royalty. (Keep in mind this was mere months before Princess Diana's death.)

While the Mel Gibson trial had hordes of swooning women lined up inside the courtroom, the Terminator attracted *everyone*. The room was standing-room only, although, typically, Schwarzenegger isn't as big as he seems onscreen. He's a big, muscular guy, no doubt, but he's only 5'10" or so—hardly a massive man-machine. He was charming and funny, and with his styled hair and a smudge of makeup on his collar, he was made for TV. But not once did I think, "Wow, that guy should be the governor someday."

The one who *did* impress me—impressed everyone, I think—was his wife. Maria Shriver is *not* a mom to mess with. A witness is not supposed to question or even address the judge directly, but she did so with such intelligence,

incisiveness, and control that he seemed awed by her. In fact, it didn't take long for her to dominate the entire courtroom; at one point, I wondered if *she* was running the trial. (I have no doubt who runs their household.)

Compare her confident dignity to the personalities of the paparazzi. They hid behind bushes, used their cars to cage a family, and called it just "doing their job."

I felt sorry for Maria and Arnold, whose fury at their child's endangerment was plain. Their family is clearly very close, and they've always done everything right—kept their kids out of the press, tried to normalize their children's lives as much as possible. An innocent trip to school turned into a mini-car chase, getting boxed in, and all because Arnold had

had heart surgery. "We felt like caged animals," Maria said.

THE VERDICT

Guilty. Harrison was sentenced to 60 days in prison, and O'Brien to 90. Seven years later, Giles Harrison seems to have learned his lesson: he was quoted in an Australian newspaper as saying, "Now, if people ask me to leave, I will. Basically, if I'm doing my job well, then nobody knows I've been anywhere near them until they open the paper."

Well, at least he leaves when they ask him to.

Unpublished Jury Sketch - Simpson Murder Trial

O.J. SIMPSON
IF THE GLOVE DOESN'T FIT...

People v. Orenthal James Simpson (1995)

Attorneys Johnnie Cochran, Marcia Clark, and Robert Shapiro at *voir dire*

Every generation has its milestones. Moments when, decades later, people recall exactly where they were and what they were doing when the news came to them: John F. Kennedy's assassination; September 11, 2001; the explosion of the Challenger. All great tragedies, these are losses that have been etched into the collective unconscious like an epitaph into a tombstone.

Bizarrely thrown in with these tragedies is June 17, 1994—the day when we dashed to the television to watch a white Bronco race up a California highway, an American hero locked inside. The story had all the elements of a blockbuster: a handsome movie and football star. His beautiful wife. A crime of passion. A highway chase scene. DNA evidence. Superstar lawyers. Murder, sex, race, cameras everywhere—the media fed the public, the public fed the media, and the nightly talk shows fed off of the case.

For almost two years, I had front row seats to the greatest show on earth.

Lawyers moved lecterns to provide a more flattering angle for the cameras, then went home to get makeovers for the next day's performance. Newscasts focused not on evidence and arguments, but on hairstyles and O.J.'s fashion choices. James Woods, Helen Mirren, and Larry King wandered into the proceedings as though they were viewing a film premiere; Annie Leibowitz photographed the proceedings *and* had private sessions with Judge Ito. Outside the doors, restaurateurs showed up with takeout and catering menus for the media, and merchandisers waved t-shirts and posters proclaiming O.J.'s guilt or innocence. When the news got out that Ito collected hourglasses, his bench turned into a display case for the timepieces.

Jury views the murder scene
on video. Note the "Ito Approved"
stamp on the illustration.

As for my end, Ito had to approve every sketch every day—no physical indication of the jury could leave his courtroom—and he stamped every piece "Ito Approved." I wanted my own keepsake, and sketched the jury surreptitiously. I've never presented it to anyone, and am now releasing it within these pages.

The entire case was theatre of the absurd, an ever-changing circus. For me, the most surreal moment came on October 3, 1995. Almost a thousand people had gathered in front of the Criminal Courts Building (later nicknamed the "Simpson Memorial Building"), the courtroom was packed to the rafters, and the 12th floor media center fell hushed and ready. While the verdict had come down the day before, after only three hours of deliberation, Ito had ordered the reading for the following morning in preparation for any violence that could break out.

At the announcement of the verdict, the media crowded in, and we were sure we knew what Ito would say. I'd seen all the same evidence, heard the same arguments, listened to the same testimony, and I was sure I knew the truth.

CAPTURED!

Judge Lance Ito surrounded by hourglasses and watching DNA testimony

THE VERDICT

Not guilty. I was floored. While cheers rose up around me—I found myself wedged between his niece and other family members—a moment of stunned silence washed over the press corps before they launched back into work. The Dream Team congratulated themselves and each other, slapping each other on the back; dancing broke out in the hallways.

The epilogue of O.J.'s story is as surreal as the rest. In late 1996, Simpson was awarded custody of his children; two months later, he's found liable for the death of their mother and Ronald Goldman in a civil trial. The Supreme Court awarded $8.5 million in compensatory damages to the Goldman family. The Dream Team lawyers—Johnnie Cochran, Robert Shapiro, F. Lee Bailey, Alan Dershowitz, and others—have gone on to varying degrees of fame beyond Simpson. Johnnie Cochran died in spring of 2005.

In the most bizarre twist, Marcia Clark—formerly professional-looking prosecuting attorney—is now working for *Entertainment Tonight,* most notably as a special correspondent on the Kobe Bryant rape trial.

The madness of the circus made it easy to forget that two people had actually *died* in a horrible fashion one night. Amid the celebrations of O.J.'s supporters, though, was a family overcome with grief: Kim Goldman, Ron Goldman's sister, moaned "Oh, my god," reminding us that she had suffered a great loss. The Goldmans, and the Simpson children, have lost their loved ones forever.

O.J. SIMPSON
SIMPSON BY THE SEA

Sharon Rufo et al., v. Orenthal James Simpson (1997)

It seemed to be only moments after the circus pulled down the tent that it rushed to the next town for an encore performance. But this show was different—the audience was smaller, but the show was so much better.

Before I get into the good stuff, you should understand the difference between civil and criminal trials. Criminal trials are sexier to the public, since the stakes are higher—freedom, possibly death, is on the line for the defendant, and the prosecution has to work hard for it, under quite a few restrictions. Civil trials aren't as sexy, because usually only money is on the line, but in my opinion, civil trials are often more fascinating. You get a lot more bang for your buck at a civil trial.

Criminal trials hold the prosecution 100% responsible for the burden of proof—they must prove to the jury,

beyond a reasonable doubt, that a defendant is guilty. Not only that, but the jury has to make a unanimous decision to convict. The Bill of Rights provides the defendant with a great deal of protection—the right to a speedy trial and counsel, protection against unreasonable search and seizure, double jeopardy, and self-incrimination. That often prevents a great deal of evidence from ever being entered into the case.

Civil trials, on the other hand, hold a defendant "liable" for a crime. The burden of proof is on the plaintiff, but the jury need only believe there's a 51% probability that the defendant committed the crime. That's a much lower standard than "beyond a reasonable doubt." In civil law, because the defendant is not considered a criminal, there is a lot less to protect them—search warrants give way to requests; the right not to incriminate one-

Denise, Juditha, and Lou Brown
watch O.J. on the stand, with photo
of Nicole showing bruises on her face

self gives way to full cooperation during depositions; public defenders are not available. That means more evidence, more testimony—more of the details that make my job so engaging. Lastly, the punishment is not taking away the defendant's freedom, but making up for the loss of the victim, usually through punitive damages. That means money. *A lot* of money.

The tenor of O.J.'s civil trial was entirely different from the criminal trial, both inside and outside the courtroom. Reason number one? Location, location, location. O.J. I, as we called it, was in the Criminal Courts Building in downtown L.A.; O.J. II was in Santa Monica, a beach town on the Westside of Los Angeles, some of the most expensive real estate in the world.

Across the street from the courthouse, the media camped out in a series of trailers in the Rand Corporation's parking lot. Some people brought in plastic flamingoes, deck and chaise lounges, and drew signs saying "Simpson By the Sea." During lunch, we either headed up to the courthouse's rooftop cafeteria view of the Pacific, or had our pick of restaurants—we spent more than a few lunch breaks walking to the Shutters Hotel on the beach, having a salad as we watched the

waves roll in, before returning to the courthouse. Even during some of the rainy, wintry weather, we could still retreat to the coziness of our trailers. Especially compared to the crowded, downtown feel of O.J. I, O.J. II was, quite

literally, a day at the beach.

Inside the courtroom was vastly different, as well. Judge Fujisaki was not keen on allowing show business to take over his courtroom. Judge Ito became a celebrity in his own right, but O.J. II saw

no cameras, kept contact with the media to a minimum, and more or less kept the circus at bay. Only one artist was allowed in the room at a time, so we had a rotating pool between the five of us—I'd draw for a week and wait another four weeks

Photographer E.J. Flammer shows copy of newspaper with his photos of O.J. wearing Bruno Magli shoes several months before the murders

Flammer with his camera and pictures of Simpson at Buffalo Bills–Miami Dolphins game on September 26, 1993

William Bodziak, F.B.I. shoeprint expert

until I stepped into the courtroom again, giving each of us about five weeks' worth of courtroom time, total. But I had plenty to draw, even outside the courtroom—Simpson came out and made speeches on the steps of the courthouse, and his most loyal fans followed him from the downtown trial.

Every trial has its "a-ha" moments, and O.J.'s "a-has" blew me away. You may have heard about the Bruno Magli shoes that were placed at the scene of the crime. Simpson said he didn't wear the "ugly-ass" size-12 Bruno Magli shoes that left footprints at the scene of the crime. Daniel Petrocelli (lawyer for Ron Goldman's family),

showed a picture of Simpson in the shoes, which Simpson said was doctored. Petrocelli brought in E.J. Flammer, a photographer who'd taken *30* photographs of Simpson in the shoes—at a Buffalo Bills game in late 1993, six months before the murders. Not only that, but he'd sold the photos to the *Buffalo Bills Report*, and held up the dated newspaper featuring the photographs of Simpson in the shoes.

Simpson's lawyer, Daniel Leonard, insisted they were all doctored, even the newspaper—and it was all for money.

Next, Petrocelli brought in two experts: a shoe expert, who identified that the shoes in the photograph were

Richard Fox shows the court the different "walls" within sock construction

the Bruno Magli shoes; and a *sock* expert to prove that the fabric in the walls of the socks would absorb blood in a particular way. *Sock experts,* I thought—people who devoted their lives to the study of sock walls?

Another big moment, for me, was when Nancy Ney took the stand. An employee at the Sojourn House for Battered Women, Ney took calls at the home's hotline. She described a call she took on the morning of June 7, 1994—five days before the murders. The woman named Nicole described her ex-husband, who'd been calling her, begging her to come back. When she went to a restaurant, she'd turn and there he'd be, staring at her. She'd go to the market, and he'd be in the next aisle; she'd look in the rearview mirror, and he'd be driving behind her. She was frightened. Not only that, but when Ney asked if she'd ever been beaten, the answer was yes—multiple times, throughout their marriage. Moreover, he'd told Nicole that if he ever saw her with another man, he'd kill her.

The most chilling part? Nicole was

Richard Fox testifies about microscopic balls of blood inside socks

calling to ask if it would be safer for her kids to just move back in with him, in order to pacify him. After some discussion, the woman decided to stay away from her ex-husband, and Ney asked that she call back the following week.

She never called back.

Simpson's lawyer spent some time demonstrating that Ney was mistaken, that it wasn't *the* Nicole, that she was merely projecting what she'd heard in the media onto the woman who'd called—that she didn't take enough notes on her call sheet to prove it was Nicole, and that her memory was faulty. But it was a big moment in the trial, no doubt—if not because of the link to the murders, then because it reminded the court that O.J. had a history of beating his wife.

Then the man himself took the stand. In the criminal trial, O.J. could not be forced to testify, but in the civil case, he had no choice. Fortunately, I was in the courtroom that week, and I waited for the moment when I could capture the case in that one image. As Petrocelli questioned Simpson about a beating incident on New Year's Eve, 1989, Simpson insisted he'd never hit Nicole (despite writings in her diary and reports from her friends that said otherwise). Pushed to the edge

CAPTURED!

by interrogation, he said he remembered what happened that night, but that he didn't know how the injuries got there—and that he felt "totally responsible" for her injuries. As Simpson evaded questions, Petrocelli asked that the photograph of Nicole's injuries be shown on the courtroom's television. She looked awful—welts and bruises and scratches covered her face. Simpson said some of the redness was normal, from Nicole's "picking" at her face.

He continued saying he "felt responsible," and even conceded that his hand may have been "on" her face. Not only that, but he had her in a headlock, trying to get her out the door. "When you say 'touched her throat,'" O.J. testified, "I was wrassling her"—*and his fists were clenched*. I nearly gasped—how many people clench their fists while describing a mild altercation with their spouses?

Finally, Petrocelli pointed at O.J. and said to the jury, "There is a killer in this courtroom, and it is O.J. Simpson." Behind him stood a television screen featuring a picture of Nicole Simpson, beaten and bruised. O.J., meanwhile, sat at his table in his glasses, sipping his water, writing on his legal pads. From my vantage point, sitting near the Goldmans and behind the Browns, I sketched furiously.

The rest of the case brought a number of O.J.'s friends, testifying that he loved his children and his wife; and other acquaintances testifying that they'd seen the couple fight. On and on it went, and I wondered the whole time, *Why didn't this come out in the criminal trial?*

THE VERDICT

Guilty. On February 4, 1997, after six days of deliberation (not five hours, like in O.J. I), the jury found O.J. Simpson liable for the deaths of Ron Goldman and Nicole Brown Simpson. They awarded $8.5 million to Goldman's parents, and $25 million in punitive damages to be shared between the Goldmans and the Browns.

But Simpson was broke, owing thousands in taxes and lawyer fees, and the courts couldn't touch his $4 million pension fund. Nicole's parents tried to get custody of her children in 2000, and lost. Simpson took his children and moved to Florida, where the state law says his earnings cannot be seized to pay damages in a civil trial; as he told a journalist, "They can't touch my earnings here. And it will be a cold day in hell before I pay a penny."

ANNA NICOLE SMITH
NONAGENARIANS PREFER BLONDES

E. Pierce Marshall v. Vickie Lynn Marshall (2001)

Anna Nicole Smith. Say the name and people inevitably roll their eyes. Her exploits have become world famous, and judging from her recent E! television show, we can look forward to a little more Anna every day.

Her initial fame was limited to the pages of magazines—she was both a *Playboy* Playmate of the Year and a Guess model—when she met oil tycoon J. Howard Marshall II. At 26, she was buxom and bodacious; at 89, he was, well, rich. He discovered the 1993 Playmate of the Year at a topless strip club called Gigi's in 1994. According to Smith, he promised her half his fortune if she would marry him. Soon after, they married in a presumably quick ceremony at a drive-in chapel in Houston.

Alas, their love was not fated to last. When Marshall died 14 months later, the young widow faced the wrath of E.

Pierce Marshall, her stepson. In his father's previous six wills, he was named as the sole heir to his father's billions, and he was not pleased when he learned that the former stripper and Playmate would inherit $474 million.

His attorney, Rusty Hardin, argued that the nonagenarian intentionally left Smith out of a living trust because he thought she was incapable of handling money, although that didn't stop him from doling out more than $6 million in jewelry, real estate, and clothing during the marriage. Hardin argued that the money was meant to make her financially independent, but by 1996—two years after she had met and married him, and less than a year after he died—she filed for bankruptcy in Los Angeles. "It costs a lot of money to be me!" was one of Smith's more memorable quotes.

As for me, I felt as though I were

back in my career as a fashion illustrator. While Smith's buxom curves looked nothing like the tall, slender fashion models I drew, wherever she went, heads swiveled. Every day, she showed up with an entourage that treated her like spun sugar: her son, her lawyers, and people

who I assume were her handlers. When she testified, I couldn't help but wonder if she had studied tapes of *Gentlemen Prefer Blondes* to prepare—her breathy voice and batting eyelashes moved so far into

Anna Nicole Smith being questioned
by her attorney, Joe Eisenberg

caricature that eventually the judge admonished her as the audience cackled. One day, she appeared wearing her hair in tight blonde curls and butterfly pins, earning the moniker "living Barbie doll."

THE VERDICT

Guilty. Plaintiff E. Pierce Marshall wins. Not only did Smith not get her inheritance, she had to pay for the court costs as well. In 2001—six years after her husband's death—a Texas probate judge ordered the former Miss Vickie Lynn Hogan to pay $541,000 in court costs to Marshall. Not only that, but Pierce's estranged brother, J. Howard III (who was also shut out of the will and sued for his share), had to pay $1.2 million in administration fees, not to mention $10 million for "filing a frivolous lawsuit." Pierce was the sole heir, leaving his brother in the dust along with his stepmother.

Smith didn't weep for long. In 2002, Los Angeles U.S. District Judge David Carter awarded her $88 million: $44.2 million in compensatory damages and an equal amount of punitive damages, finding that Pierce had spied on her and interfered with her inheritance.

As a result of her newfound fame, she landed *The Anna Nicole Show* on the E! network, now available on DVD. She's also suing for $30 million in interest she claims she's owed for the time that she *didn't* have the $88 million settlement.

E. Pierce Marshall, on the other hand, is still on the Forbes 400 list. He's appealing the Los Angeles settlement, so I expect to be seeing both of them soon. Here's a judgment call—who's greedier? The millionaire who wants more millions, or the millionaire who wants more millions?

Anna Nicole with her son, while constantly being comforted by her entourage

LINDA SOBEK
LOST IN THE DESERT

People v. Charles Rathbun (1996)

Many of you may not have heard of Linda Sobek. Like so many Americans who dream of a life among the rich and famous, she died before she could become immortalized in the hearts of the world. Her death still haunts me.

The pretty, 27-year-old model was a former Los Angeles Raider cheerleader and part-time model who aimed to become a full-time fashion model. In late November, 1995, Charles Rathbun, who made his living creating "cheesecake-and-car" photographs for auto magazines, offered her a career opportunity: a fashion shoot for *Motor Trend Magazine*. As she happily told her family, she would be posing in the wilderness of the Angeles National Forest for a national publication.

No one heard from her again. A week after the shoot, Charles Rathbun led the police to her shallow grave,

telling them he accidentally hit her with the SUV with which she was supposed to have posed (he said he was doing "donut" car stunts in the desert). He claimed he then panicked and buried her. Authorities doubted his story, especially since her injuries were not consistent with an auto accident. He was arrested and tried a year later.

I don't know if it was my history sketching fashion models, the suffocating grief of the families, or just the gruesome details, but I suffered nightmares for months after the trial. The images of the pretty young woman could've been any model I knew, somewhat naïve and always optimistic and ambitious. I couldn't reconcile that with the graphic, grisly photos of her body—severe rope burns on her legs, and evidence of strangulation, rape, and sodomy. Her family was desperate with grief, and his family

Charles Rathbun on the witness stand.
Behind him are his photos of Linda Sobek
in unusual garb for a fashion scene.

Sobek's parents listen to painful testimony

expressed only measured anger and indignance.

The evidence that disturbs me to this day, though, were his photos of her that day in the desert. She wore a sheer, flower-print dress and white sandals—perfect for a sunny day in southern California—but she also wore torn black thigh-high stockings. Why, I wondered, would any fashion photographer make such a choice? Were they his idea of fashion? Were those stockings responsible for the ligature marks? She didn't smile in any of the photographs, and I couldn't help but wonder if she had been forced to wear the stockings, if fear had settled into her heart, if she already sensed that coming to the desert that day would be the last choice she would ever make.

THE VERDICT

Guilty. Rathbun maintained his innocence, but between his inconsistent stories and the piles of evidence, he was sentenced to life in prison. Leading investigators to her body saved him from execution, but not from punishment.

Since Sobek's death, modeling agencies have become more vigilant about photographers and their models' whereabouts, but they still place a great responsibility on the women to be careful about their assignments. Whatever happened that day in the forest, Linda Sobek's case was another tragic story of an eager, pretty girl who went searching for fame and never came back.

Defense attorney Mark Werksman
and Prosecutor Stephen Kay watch
police investigator's demonstration

Prosecutor Stephen Kay questions witness
about rolls of film, while attorney Mark
Werksman and Charles Rathbun look on

Charles Rathbun's family in sharp
contrast to the family of Sobek

Steven Spielberg animatedly
testifies at stalking trial

Jonathan Norman stares at
Spielberg during the stalking trial

STEVEN SPIELBERG CLOSE ENCOUNTERS OF THE STALKER KIND

People v. Jonathan Norman (1998)

Sometimes, the public eye can feel more like the laser beam sight on a rifle. I've had my brushes with fame—I've even appeared in films and television—and I enjoyed it thoroughly. But Steven Spielberg, king of American cinema, made me grateful that I'm not a superstar.

In 1997, police arrested Jonathan Norman for breaking and entering the grounds of Spielberg's home. At the time, Spielberg and his family were on location, shooting *Saving Private Ryan*. Norman had not only trespassed on his property *three* other times that year, but this time, he brought a rape kit with him—hand-

Attorneys looking at security
footage at the Spielberg home

cuffs, an Exacto knife, duct tape, and razor blades. During the trial, prosecutors painted a picture of a disturbed young man who planned to tie up Spielberg's wife, Kate Capshaw, and force her to watch him rape the director.

On the stand, Spielberg seemed terrified. He refused to look at the defendant, gave terse, defiant answers, and couldn't get out of the courtroom fast enough. He was the object of Norman's mission, he said, and the defendant

wouldn't stop until he had carried it out. I've never seen such a frightened witness.

Norman, on the other hand, was visibly delighted to have Spielberg in the same room with him. Spielberg's fear seemed to feed his joy; for the first time, the predator could smell his prey's terror.

THE VERDICT

Guilty. Conviction of felony stalking usually carries a minimum term of four years, but California's three-strikes law and two prior convictions guaranteed Norman 25 years to life in prison. Spielberg went on to win an Oscar for directing *Saving Private Ryan*.

CAPTURED!

HUNTER TYLO
THE BOLD, THE BEAUTIFUL, AND THE BABIES

Hunter Tylo v. Aaron Spelling (1996)

Tylo watches proceedings

Art imitates life. And sometimes, art imitates life that imitates art that was imitating life. Such was the delightfully strange story of Hunter Tylo's trial in 1997.

Before we get to the real trial, a bit of backstory: In 1997, I was hired to play a courtroom artist during a trial on *The Bold and the Beautiful.* Go figure. *The Bold and the Beautiful,* as I'm sure you know, is a world-renowned daytime soap opera, and, at 450 million people in 98 countries, was the most-watched show on earth. I loved the idea of experiencing the world of the soap opera from the inside out, and hey, who wouldn't like to get their 15 minutes on such a big stage?

Every day for several weeks, I showed up at 7:00 A.M. for makeup, and I spent more time there than I did onscreen. Layers of makeup caked on my face, my hair teased into an impossibly shellacked bouffant, my hands lovingly made up, as well—I like looking good as much as the next woman, but I felt like I was suffocating under so many chemicals. But I wouldn't trade it for the world; I got an inside scoop on the bizarre and secretive subculture of soap operas.

The conversation flowed constantly and consistently: soap operas, diets, who's working out with what trainer. Those were the primary topics. I'm used to being surrounded by journalists and lawyers, people who make a living thinking about the world, politics, and occasionally Michael Jackson's hairpiece, but for several weeks, all I heard about were soap operas, diets, and trainers; I also looked on in disbelief as no one ate anything, ever.

It's no wonder the world is so insular, though; time moves at an altered speed in soap opera land. Not to mention the fans, of course; I'd never have recognized most of the actors on "*B&B*," but I got *fan mail* as a result of my stint, and I didn't even cry on command. All I did was my real-life job with more makeup. I once met a woman in a hair salon who was visiting town for a *Days of Our Lives* convention, and when I mentioned my time on *B&B*, her eyes lit up as though I were the Holy Mother.

With so much time to kill during the takes, I noticed patterns: long, lingering looks before every commercial break. The extraordinary ability to weep copious tears at the drop of a hat. Long-running characters that disappeared and were replaced without fanfare. And the flowers! *B&B* is very proud of their real flower arrangements—no fakes, delivered daily, one of those touches that set them apart as a classy soap.

I won't get into the details of the trial itself (you would need a flowchart to follow all the relationships), but in a nutshell, Ridge and Grant were both in love with Brooke. Grant falsely accused Ridge of shooting him. Ridge was arrested. Ridge's fiancée was Taylor. Taylor was played by Hunter Tylo.

Hunter's character was a witness at the *B&B* trial, and because we sat next to each other, we got to be friendly. Imagine my surprise when, six months later, I found myself sketching her in a real courtroom.

Tylo left her role as Dr. Taylor Forrester to play Victoria "Taylor" Davis McBride on the hit show *Melrose Place* (apparently she looks like a Taylor). Taylor was a vengeful vixen, and when Tylo revealed she was pregnant, Aaron Spelling, the producer of the program, sacked her—vixens are sexy, and pregnant women aren't sexy. Tylo sued.

Few trials match this one for sheer ugliness—not to mention sex appeal. Lisa Rinna, the large-lipped wife of Harry Hamlin, who took on the role of Taylor after Tylo was fired, testified to say she had to play her sexuality to the hilt. Heather Locklear showed up in a midriff top and painted-on jeans, oversized bottle of Evian in tow, to talk about sex

appeal. Even with the camera's extra ten pounds, both women were rail-thin. Meanwhile, the slender, but pregnant, Tylo, heard again and again how very unsexy she was.

When Tylo mentioned that other actresses, like Julia Louis-Dreyfuss, hid their pregnancies on the set, the defense retorted that Elaine's not supposed to be sexy—she's a comedic actress, so she can be unappealing to men. And meanwhile, I'm sketching away, with Tylo and I reminiscing about the kinder, gentler attempted murder trial we had fictionalized only months before.

THE VERDICT

Guilty. Aaron Spelling paid $5,000,000 to Tylo; naturally, he's appealing. Meanwhile, the baby who was the focus of the trial was born with a deadly eye cancer, retinoblastoma, and Tylo helped pass California State Bill AB218, which provides all infants in California with pupil dilation for detection of preventable forms of blindness and fatal diseases. Tylo, a devout Christian, also wrote a bestselling autobiography and frequently goes on speaking tours to support her nonprofit organization, Hunter's Chosen Child. Her most recent acting gig was a role on Sci-Fi Network's *Hammerhead:*

Shark Frenzy, and she's back on *The Bold and the Beautiful.*

Melrose Place, of course, went off the air in 1999, and Aaron Spelling continues to crank out evening soap operas.

And how's this for irony: In 1998, a very pregnant Lisa Rinna posed nude in *Playboy* magazine.

Tylo watches as her attorney questions TV show executive on hiring policy

CAPTURED!

LESLIE VAN HOUTEN
CHARLIE'S GIRL, MODEL PRISONER

Leslie Van Houten Parole Hearing (2002)

How long does it take to make up for the sins of youth? For the Manson girls, a lifetime. Every few years, Leslie van Houten is trotted out for another parole hearing, and each time, it's denied; the same goes for the other women who carried out Manson's grisly bidding in the summer of 1969. When I attended Leslie's parole hearing in 2002, one thought kept coursing through my mind: *what a waste of her life.*

I don't suppose I have to remind you of the Manson murders, but here's Leslie's part in it. On August 9, 1989, a group of Manson's devotees descended on the home of actress Sharon Tate and murdered her and four of her friends: coffee heiress Abigail Folger and her boyfriend Voytek Frykowski; Jay Sebring, internationally renowned hairstylist; and Steve Parent, a teenager who had come to visit Tate's caretaker. Tate was eight months pregnant at the time.

Later that night, another group broke into the home of Leo and Rosemary LaBianca and murdered them, as well. The 19-year-old Leslie van Houten—the youngest of the Manson girls—was in this second group. While there's some confusion about whether she murdered Rosemary LaBianca, the fact that she stabbed her 14 to 16 times is a matter of record. (Leslie says Charles "Tex" Watson killed Rosemary before Leslie stabbed her.) In 1972, she was convicted of murder and sentenced to die; when the Supreme Court overturned the death penalty in 1973, her sentence was commuted to life.

At her parole hearing, she was a 52-year-old beautiful woman with the bearing of a mythical mother figure: ethereal, statuesque, and peaceful. "My heart aches and there seems to be no way to convey the amount of pain I caused," she proclaimed. "I don't know what else to say. "She wore no make-up, of course, and looked remarkably young, despite the long gray braid that draped over her shoulder. I suppose being a model prisoner must be a fairly stress-free life—with no surprises, no children, and no possessions, her primary concern is filling time. She's earned two college degrees, completed all available prison self-improvement programs, and assisted other inmates in doing the same. But is that enough?

For her fans, it is. I was stunned by her enormous fan club—conservatively dressed types, hippies, bohemians; they came from every walk of life and every corner of the country to show their support for Leslie, whom they believe has paid her dues. But also in attendance were relatives of the LaBiancas, who voiced strong opposition, given the particular brutality of the crime.

THE VERDICT

Parole denied. Leslie didn't cry during the hearing. The judge was terse, proper, and old-fashioned, and in a courtroom that looked like it was built a century earlier, he refused her parole. I couldn't help but think of how Manson had taken her life, too—drugs and his influence had led her to one horrible, tragic decision as a kid, and her life's been spent behind bars, making up for it. If it hadn't been for him, she would probably be a grandmother by now. Instead, she's back to life as a model prisoner.

Zeta-Jones tearfully recounts fears after receiving a "funeral announcement" from stalker Dawnette Knight

Michael Douglas demonstrates controlled rage from the witness stand

CATHERINE ZETA-JONES A SCHOOLGIRL CRUSH

People v. Dawnette Knight (2005)

Some actors are disappointing when you see them in person. They're small, or balding, or have bad skin, or any of the other thousand physical traits that make them as human as you are.

Catherine Zeta-Jones was *not* one of those people. Not even close. She's not human so much as a walking, talking Hollywood glamour goddess.

So I can see why someone might see her as a threat. Especially Dawnette Knight, a young woman with a "girlish crush" on Zeta-Jones's husband, Michael Douglas.

Like any woman with a weakness for a strong jawline, she began a letter-writing campaign describing why, when, and how she planned to remove the wife from the picture. While she didn't boil any bunnies—and, yes, I had to go there—she was a dedicated woman, writing over two dozen letters to Zeta-Jones.

She even wrote to Douglas himself, subscribing to the age-old adage that the way to a man's heart is to slice and dice his wife into tiny pieces. The letters included comparisons to Sharon Tate, meat on a bone and dog food; what man wouldn't leave a glamour goddess for a creative spirit like that?

Knight wasn't content to write letters, of course. At one point, she called Zeta-Jones at her hotel in Holland and described Zeta-Jones's itinerary, hotel hallway, and the seven minutes between the movie star and her impending death.

Just a girlish crush, really.

Originally, Knight faced 24 counts of making criminal threats and one count of stalking; 21 of the former counts were later dropped. After a short delay (Knight overdosed on barbiturates at one point), I was treated to the sight of Catherine Zeta-Jones in court.

Not only is Catherine Zeta-Jones extraordinarily beautiful in person, she also has the confidence and charm of a woman who knows her effect on others and uses it when necessary. Dressed in a plain black cotton knit dress and black sandals, simple watch, and that mane of hair falling softly around her shoulders, she was the picture of demure sanity. Contrast that with Knight, who had bad hair extensions, a sweater made of rabbit fur, and blue overalls. The stalker didn't have a chance. (At one point, I saw a guard take the rabbit sweater from Knight; he carried it between his thumb and forefinger, at arm's length.)

When Zeta-Jones took the stand, she may as well have been climbing the steps to accept her Oscar. She spoke in that lovely, throaty voice, that lilting Welsh accent, in such a tired, weary manner; she wept; she became breathless with anxiety. I don't doubt she honestly felt anxious—she sat in a room with the woman who had promised to make mincemeat out of her, literally—but I couldn't help but wonder how much of her testimony was Catherine Zeta-Jones, victim, and how much was Catherine Zeta-Jones, Oscar winner.

Douglas, on the other hand, seemed 100% genuine on the stand, and his sincerity didn't bode well for his psycho sycophant. He looked great, of course—very elegant in a custom-tailored gray suit—but I wouldn't have liked to be the object of his ire. He *seethed*, furious that anyone had made his wife feel such anxiety, let alone make her weep so. I think he would have strangled Knight if he had gotten close enough to her. One thing I learned from that trial: Michael Douglas is truly, madly in love with his wife.

The weirdest part? Knight had a boyfriend. Sitting in the courtroom with her, a regular software developer who said his girlfriend didn't really mean any harm, he watched as her victims paraded across the stand, describing every manner of "Satanic" threats, as Zeta-Jones called it. He even gave out business cards to the media. For all I know, they're still together.

THE VERDICT

No contest. Knight pleaded no contest to one felony count of stalking and three felony counts of making criminal threats. She underwent psychiatric testing to determine whether she should get probation or up to five years behind bars; in July 2005, she was sentenced to three years in prison.

BOOKS AVAILABLE FROM SANTA MONICA PRESS

www.santamonicapress.com • 1-800-784-9553

American Hydrant
by Sean Crane
176 pages $24.95

**Atomic Wedgies, Wet Willies &
Other Acts of Roguery**
by Greg Tananbaum and Dan Martin
128 pages $11.95

The Bad Driver's Handbook
*Hundreds of Simple Maneuvers to Frustrate,
Annoy, and Endanger Those Around You*
by Zack Arnstein and Larry Arnstein
192 pages $12.95

The Butt Hello
and other ways my cats drive me crazy
by Ted Meyer
96 pages $9.95

Calculated Risk
The Extraordinary Life of Jimmy Doolittle
by Jonna Doolittle Hoppes
360 pages $24.95

Can a Dead Man Strike Out?
*Offbeat Baseball Questions
and Their Improbable Answers*
by Mark S. Halfon
192 pages $11.95

Childish Things
by Davis & Davis
96 pages $19.95

The Dog Ate My Resumé
by Zack Arnstein and Larry Arnstein
192 pages $11.95

Dogme Uncut
*Lars von Trier, Thomas Vinterberg
and the Gang That Took on Hollywood*
by Jack Stevenson
312 pages $16.95

Elvis Presley Passed Here
*Even More Locations of America's
Pop Culture Landmarks*
by Chris Epting
336 pages $16.95

Exotic Travel Destinations for Families
by Jennifer M. Nichols and Bill Nichols
360 pages $16.95

5,000 Reasons to Smile . . . for Chicks
by Sally DeLellis
240 pages $11.95

Footsteps in the Fog
Alfred Hitchcock's San Francisco
by Jeff Kraft and Aaron Leventhal
240 pages $24.95

French for Le Snob
Adding Panache to Your Everyday Conversations
by Yvette Reche
400 pages $16.95

Haunted Hikes
*Spine-Tingling Tales and Trails from North
America's National Parks*
by Andrea Lankford
312 pages $16.95

How to Speak Shakespeare
by Cal Pritner and Louis Colaianni
144 pages $16.95

**Jackson Pollock:
Memories Arrested in Space**
by Martin Gray
216 pages $14.95

James Dean Died Here
*The Locations of America's
Pop Culture Landmarks*
by Chris Epting
312 pages $16.95

The Keystone Kid
Tales of Early Hollywood
by Coy Watson, Jr.
312 pages $24.95

L.A. Noir
The City as Character
by Alain Silver and James Ursini
176 pages $19.95

Loving Through Bars
Children with Parents in Prison
by Cynthia Martone
216 pages $21.95

Marilyn Monroe Dyed Here
*More Locations of America's
Pop Culture Landmarks*
by Chris Epting
312 pages $16.95

Movie Star Homes
by Judy Artunian and Mike Oldham
312 pages $16.95

My So-Called Digital Life
*2,000 Teenagers, 300 Cameras,
and 30 Days to Document Their World*
by Bob Pletka
176 pages $24.95

Offbeat Museums
*The Collections and Curators
of America's Most Unusual Museums*
by Saul Rubin
240 pages $19.95

A Prayer for Burma
by Kenneth Wong
216 pages $14.95

Quack!
*Tales of Medical Fraud from
the Museum of Questionable Medical Devices*
by Bob McCoy
240 pages $19.95

Redneck Haiku
Double-Wide Edition
by Mary K. Witte
240 pages $11.95

**The Ruby Slippers, Madonna's Bra,
and Einstein's Brain**
The Locations of America's Pop Culture Artifacts
by Chris Epting
312 pages $16.95

**School Sense: How to Help Your Child
Succeed in Elementary School**
by Tiffani Chin, Ph.D.
408 pages $16.95

Silent Echoes
*Discovering Early Hollywood
Through the Films of Buster Keaton*
by John Bengtson
240 pages $24.95

Tiki Road Trip
A Guide to Tiki Culture in North America
by James Teitelbaum
288 pages $16.95